NICE GUYS FINISH LAST

Management Myths and Reality

Lawrence L. Steinmetz, Ph.D.

Horizon Publications, Inc.
Boulder, Colorado 80301

Distributed by:
DEVIN-ADAIR, PUBLISHERS
Old Greenwich, CT 06870

*For information contact Horizon Publications, Inc., 3333 Iris Ave., Boulder,
Colorado 80301 or Devin-Adair, Publishers, Box A, Old Greenwich, CT 06870*

Cover design: Brent Beck/Fifth Street Design
Text design: Marilyn Langfeld
Copy editor: Julie Segedy
Composition: HMS Typography, Inc.
Printed in the United States of America.

Library of Congress Cataloging in Publication Data

Steinmetz, Lawrence L.
  Nice guys finish last.

      1.   Industrial management.   2.   Personnel management.
3.   Success.   I.   Title.
HD31.S6924   1983   658   83-5264
ISBN 0-8159-6316-5

83 84 85 86 5 4 3 2 1

Contents

Foreword

In dedicating this book to George Odiorne, Larry Steinmetz has given formal recognition to two dimensions of George's contribution. One is well known. It is his contribution to the field of management.

Odiorne's ideas have permeated and even shaped the way American business thinks about and engages in the process of management. His writings—the hundreds of articles and many books—have touched on virtually every aspect of individual and organizational leadership. He is perhaps best known for taking the concept of management by objectives and turning it into a viable system of management that is now operable, in some form, in nearly every American company, government agency and service organization.

Tens of thousands of executives and managers have heard George Odiorne in university seminars, in-company management development programs or at conferences. He is, by almost any standard, a master of his trade. Known for his dynamic style and straightforward, unvarnished language, he succeeds in winning an audience as well as educating it.

The humor which so often punctuates his presentations is based not on a repertoire of after-dinner jokes but rather on his ability to see and share with his audience the silliness of organizational life. He loves to poke fun at finger-pointing bureaucrats caught up on the treadmill of quarterly reports, at self-important executives who isolate themselves in the corporate grandeur of thick carpets and oak paneled offices, and at pompous academics whose abstruse theories test how many vice presidents can sit on the head of a matrix.

Many a listener identifies quickly with the situations Odiorne describes. ''That's my company he's talking about,'' they'll say. Others squirm as they see themselves among the characters he depicts. But the depth of his criticism is greater than the humor or discomfort of an anecdote might suggest.

His writings and oral presentations, which seemingly focus on the "how to do it" of management, are undergirded by thoughtful and far-ranging analyses of the individual, the organization, and society. For example, George can lay out in diagrammatic fashion the elements of compensation administration. Even the novice can easily perceive the inter-relationship of these elements and can use them to calculate the wage rate for a typist or the benefits package for a divisional general manager. There is almost an insert-tab-A-in-slot-B clarity about the procedure he prescribes. It is possible though to use the procedure in an unthinking way, to presume that the mechanics of the task are more important than the results to which they lead. Odiorne doesn't permit this. He raises fundamental questions that the less thoughtful so often ignore or fail even to see. He asks "how much is an executive worth?" and treats the question as one that requires more than an arithmetic solution. The calculation must include moral, psychological, political, and social values as well as economic ones.

Those who would cope with this more difficult, demanding task can find ample and helpful guidance in his writings. They will also find an author whose interests and insights go far beyond those of his more parochial professional colleagues. For example, a 1969 book, *Green Power: The Corporation and the Urban Crisis*, is as much a tract on social policy as it is on how to develop a minority hiring program. A 1967 paper, "Are the Intellectual and the Corporation Compatible?", raises an apparently abstract philosophical issue that turns out to be a "practical" one for scholar and executive alike. As this paper illustrates, Odiorne's readers/listeners invariably get more than they bargain for. Those who want only the answers—the how-to-do-its of management—are confronted with the questions as well. And those who find comfort in dealing only with concepts, theories or models are prodded to take these ideas and turn them into actions.

I have alluded here to Odiorne's two contributions and described one of them—his contribution to the development of management thought. His second contribution is a more personal and, for me, more appreciated one. It is his contribution to the development of people. I am one of them. Larry Steinmetz, this book's author is another. We are only two of hundreds and perhaps thousands whose lives have been touched directly by George's guidance, support, encouragement, generosity, and, sometimes, kick in the seat of the pants. He has not only the ability but the desire to help people succeed. In the jargon of Abraham Maslow's Hierachy of Needs, George helps people to self-actualize, to realize their full potential.

Many of those he has helped were his students at the University of Michigan where he taught for ten years. Other beneficiaries include his faculty colleagues at Michigan, the University of Utah, and, more recently at the University of Massachusetts. Still others include would-be entrepreneurs who lacked the skills (or the capital) to turn their hopes into a going business. Not infrequently, George gave them both.

As his students we were often dumbfounded by how he taught. He was like few professors we had encountered in our academic careers. While he could have relied on lecturing—he was superb at it—he chose instead to put us to work. He sent us off to libraries to unearth information. He created publications and had us serve as writers or editors. He got companies or government agencies to fund research projects and sent us out into the world to seek out the truth. He turned us into student consultants, working with local companies to solve problems that our textbooks told us were easy to solve. Not surprisingly, our out-of-the-classroom learning equipped us with skills and experiences that more traditional techniques could only approximate and later in our careers we were able to capitalize handsomely on those tasks to which he had set us.

As these comments suggest, ours was not the typical student-professor relationship. Instead of intoning at us, he brought us into his arena. We worked with him; we were his colleagues, his co-authors and, it seemed sometimes, his conspirators in a collection of intellectual enterprises that were as much fun as they were educational. His Ph.D. students, usually relegated to teaching a section of an introductory undergraduate course, were brought into the School's management development programs as junior lecturers. This early career exposure to executives and the real-world attitude they held, enabled these fledging academics to develop a sense of balance that is sometimes never gained by the young scholar who is instead permitted or encouraged to burrow into the library stacks, insulating him or herself from the world of the practitioner.

The beneficiaries of George's help constitute a modest who's who in academia and industry. Many have ascended to officer-level positions in major corporations. Some are owners and CEO's of their own firms. Those who chose academic careers have themselves made important contributions to the field of management and have distinguished themselves as teachers, consultants and scholars. While their success is undoubtedly a consequence of their own abilities and efforts, it is equally apparent that these people can ascribe more than a modicum of their achievements to George's influence.

Larry's book has two purposes. First, it is designed to help its readers understand and practice management better. Having read through the manuscript, I am sure it will fulfill that purpose. Its second purpose, implicit in the book's dedication and the preceding paragraphs, is to say thank you to George Odiorne. We all appreciate how he has helped us. I am particularly grateful for being given the opportunity to express the affection and gratitude that so many of us have for our mentor and friend.

Albert W. Schrader
Associate Dean for
Management Education
Graduate School of Business Administration
The University of Michigan

Preface

Why would anybody write a book with chapter titles nothing more than platitudes and bromides? The answer is that one gets an idea into his head that some things are true which are not believed and some things are believed which are not true.

In my many years of experience as a consultant and management educator, I have repeatedly heard assertions about what is right and what is wrong about and in the world. These assertions are practically always amusing, sometimes astonishing, but invariably either interesting or boring, depending upon the situation from which they emerge.

One day, after having a string of days in which various statements and sayings were offered to me as fact, the idea occurred to me that I certainly have not been the first, nor will I be the last individual to try to educate people in management about how to better operate their organization. And, being a management educator, it seemed important that I pass along at least some of my thoughts about some of these beliefs. Whether they are accurate or not, they might provide some food for future generations of management educators and managers. Therefore, I thought I might share some of my observations which I have accumulated over the years in the form of a book.

While writing this book, I began to realize that the only reason that I am in the business of management education is because of a series of accidents—all of them beneficial—and largely a consequence of interfaces and interrelationships which I have had with a series of people in my lifetime.

Perhaps the most beneficial accident, which started me in the direction of management education, was encountering George S. Odiorne, who, at the time, was a professor at the Graduate School of Business at the University of Michigan while I was working on my Ph.D. After deciding to return to Graduate School, I sent twenty-two letters to institutions of higher education inquiring about their Ph.D. programs, but the

University of Michigan was not included in this select list. However, my wife, Sally, sent a letter there anyway, mainly because her uncle, Dr. Claude W. Hibbard, was a University of Michigan paleontology professor.

Making a long story short, I ended up at the University of Michigan largely on the strength of a letter which George Odiorne wrote me in reply to my (wife's) letter. Charisma is an interesting thing. And George Odiorne's charisma can come through a letter (not as effectively as it does personally, but nevertheless, it does come through).

I had never thought much about management education until I met George Odiorne. His enthusiasm is contagious and in less than a year, I knew this was the direction I wanted to take professionally. It is for this reason that this book is dedicated to George S. Odiorne.

Subsequent to George Odiorne, there have been several people in my life I've met and worked with who have also been a part of the series of beneficial accidents: Clark C. Caskey, Richard J. Nachman, R.G.T. Millar, Alan Filley, and Charles D. Greenidge have all had a very beneficial effect in shaping and directing my thoughts and ideas as a management educator.

And then there were the entrepreneurs. Since most of my professional career has been spent educating and consulting with entrepreneurial people, I feel that it is worthwhile mentioning several individual executives who really helped solidify my respect for and belief in executives who really make things happen in our society. There's no particular order to these individuals—in fact, in some cases, I can't even remember when I first met them. But they all had a profound impact on my ideas about management in one way or another. And to the extent that this book has any decent ideas in it for future generations of management, all of the foregoing individuals must be thanked as well as the following: Thomas T. Bernstein, Sr., Frederick G. Wacker, Jr., Burt Bliss, Tom Holce, and literally hundreds of other executives and managers from a broad diversity of companies throughout the United States.

To all the foregoing individuals, I hope this book is some kind of tribute but, specifically, I hope that it is a tribute to George S. Odiorne. To the degree that there is anything good and right about this book, I'd like to blame it on these inspirational people for giving me those ideas. I hope it reflects favorably on the impact that they have had on me in my thinking, and I would like to thank each and every one of them for making this book a contribution to the lore of management in, hopefully, some constructive way.

Lawrence L. Steinmetz
Boulder, Colorado
April, 1983

I

Truth

1

"Ain't It So, Lefty?"

This book is about truth—or what is often alleged to be true. Most managers of people and organizations believe in certain God-given, inalienable bits of true wisdom. They also believe that these "truths" guide them in their quest for success in running all organizations—large or small, government or private industry, manufacturing, retailing, wholesaling, construction, or service oriented. These "truths," which successful managers feel they must adhere to, have evolved from a body of lore that over the years has been developed, refined, reinforced, and reinvented.

Almost everyone agrees with at least some of these "truths." Remember the old movie character who would support the "truth" of his statements by turning to his sidekick with the verifying question, "Ain't it so, Lefty?" Lefty, of course, was guaranteed to swear to it, so doubters never even questioned the authenticity of the facts, figures, or testimony that had just been made.

In a similar vein, many managers try to authenticate their managerial practices today. When they have found themselves unsuccessful in interpersonal relationships and/or the conduct of their businesses, they are frustrated because they've abided by the tenets of the trade. Unfortunately these truths have been taught and reinforced by so many "knowledgeable" persons that the recipients long ago gave up even questioning whether the statements were valid—or even relevant to current situations.

Here's how one of these fundamental "truths" can affect a manager's behavior and ultimate success (or failure).

If You Want a Job Done Right, Do It Yourself

We've all heard the adage, "If you want a job done right, do it yourself." The reason for this is obvious: If you do it yourself, you know it is done the way you want it done. Furthermore, you know if a problem comes up, the most responsible person in the world (you) is there to handle it; you also know that if it doesn't come out right, then because the most knowledgeable, competent person in the world was doing it, it could not have been done any better.

Experienced executives know the pitfalls of this so-called truism. Anyone who believes it is by definition unable to delegate—the very hallmark of an effective manager.

There are also variations of the "If you want a job done right, do it yourself" idea. Probably the most prevalent is, "Don't send a boy (girl) to do a man's (woman's) job." This statement is often used to put down others (particularly younger people) in the organization, but many people who feel their talents and skills are superior to others still believe it.

How Much Truth Do You Believe?

So, this book is about myths, paradoxes, truths, realities, and anachronisms in management. It is not designed to destroy belief in fundamental truths, but to check out the real relevance and practicality of believing in conventional wisdoms. The facts are that much conventional wisdom doesn't actually work very well in practice—a situation that creates any number of problems for supervisors and managers attempting to get results through people. Yet, at times, many of these truths seem to work—and work well. So what is one to believe?

How do you feel about many of these managerial truths? The following test is a quick checklist to see how you manage.

Grab a pencil and take the test before you read the rest of the book. The opinions you have now may very well change by the time you have finished the final chapter.

Managerial Truth Test

Indicate the degree or extent of the "truth" stated on the left by checking the appropriate response on the right. Keep in mind that there is no right or wrong answer.

	Always	Usually	Seldom	Practically Never
1. If you want a job done right, do it yourself.	_____	_____	_____	_____
2. Hard work never hurt anyone.	_____	_____	_____	_____
3. Idle hands are the workshop of the Devil.	_____	_____	_____	_____
4. You shouldn't ask someone to do something you can't do yourself.	_____	_____	_____	_____
5. Do unto others as you would have others do unto you.	_____	_____	_____	_____
6. The open-door policy is a good rule for any manager to follow.	_____	_____	_____	_____
7. Nice guys finish last.	_____	_____	_____	_____
8. A good boss is a person who is a good human relator.	_____	_____	_____	_____
9. To do something right takes time.	_____	_____	_____	_____
10. If one wants to get ahead, one needs a college education.	_____	_____	_____	_____
11. Good workers make good supervisors.	_____	_____	_____	_____
12. Your best worker is your best trainer.	_____	_____	_____	_____

	Always	Usually	Seldom	Practically Never
13. A good boss will always take an interest in his/her employees.	_____	_____	_____	_____
14. A highly motivated worker is more effective than one who is not.	_____	_____	_____	_____
15. Employees' attitude is what counts.	_____	_____	_____	_____
16. If you can't say anything good about someone, don't say anything at all.	_____	_____	_____	_____
17. People rise to their level of incompetence.	_____	_____	_____	_____
18. Blackmail is bad—and so is bribery.	_____	_____	_____	_____
19. The best way to motivate people is to pay them by commission.	_____	_____	_____	_____
20. One has a tough time competing when the competition keeps cutting your price.	_____	_____	_____	_____
21. We sell below cost, but we can make it up in volume.	_____	_____	_____	_____
22. The demand curve for any product slopes downward and to the right.	_____	_____	_____	_____
23. You can afford to sell cheaper to the large quantity buyer.	_____	_____	_____	_____
24. Production costs go down as production volume goes up.	_____	_____	_____	_____
25. What really counts in business is the "bottom line."	_____	_____	_____	_____
26. We're going to finance our growth from the earnings of our business.	_____	_____	_____	_____

If you thought that most of the above statements are usually or practically always applicable in operating a business, you might want to reevaluate your current position. Practically all these statements have questionable appropriateness in management and supervision.

II

Truth in Managing Yourself

2

If You Want A Job Done Right, Do It Yourself

The statement "If you want a job done right, do it yourself" has been said so many times and reinforced by a deliberate, affirmative nod of the listener's head that it is very difficult for some of us seriously to question its appropriateness.

The idea of attaining perfection by doing a job yourself stems essentially from your dissatisfaction with the way someone else does it, or your impatience while waiting for someone else to do it. But what does it mean to "do a job right"?

What Is Right?

Whenever anyone does a job, there's always the possibility that it will be done well or poorly. But the value of "done well" can vary. Consider, for example, the parent who tells a child to wash the pots and pans used to prepare dinner. Obviously, the parent wants the child to do a good job—that is, clean the pots and pans. But exactly how do you decide whether a pot or pan is clean? Do you establish standards of "reflectiveness" as seen in some television commercials for soaps and detergents? And if there is an arbitrary standard that is quantifiable and meaningful, how do you know whether that standard is realistic? It may be that the parent sets higher standards than are needed for good health, or than the child feels is reasonable, or even than the parent would set for himself or herself when performing the same task.

In the same way, any superior who assigns a job to a subordinate has an extremely difficult chore: establishing some criteria for acceptability. Instead of creating meaningful standards that can be observed, measured, and substantiated, many bosses would rather simply do the job themselves. It's easier than trying to train or evaluate a subordinate. And, subordinates don't get the chance to complain that certain standards are unrealistic, certain functions unnecessary, or certain methods outdated.

Usually the Boss Can't Do It Better Anyway

Many bosses do the job themselves because they do not want to have to make an adequate, meaningful job assignment. But more importantly, approximately 80 percent of the time when bosses claim they can do the job better, they really mean, "I can do the job better to *suit myself.*"

It's very difficult to measure the quality of one's work. It's usually easier to measure quantity—just count how much is done. It is also easier to ascertain whether a job was done on schedule or within budget. But measuring the qualitative performance of a job poses certain difficulties. How do you ascertain the quality of a written report or of a training session or of a sale that was made or of a presentation to an executive committee?

People undertake jobs themselves instead of delegating in the belief that they can do the job better than the subordinate. Yet studies show that bosses' results do not measure any higher by any objective criteria. Granted, the job was done *as well as* what the subordinate probably would have done—but there is no reason to believe that it was actually done better.

But Sometimes the Boss Can Do It Better

In some cases, however, the boss can do the job better. Let's assume that everyone in the whole world, even the boss's in-laws, agree that the boss can do the job better than anyone else. That is still *not* a reason for the boss to persist in doing the job. *Even if* he or she can do it better, there is still every argument to delegate or assign the task to a subordinate, at least when it is possible that the subordinate can do the job *well enough*.

Good Enough Is Really the Delegation Criterion

When a job is delegated, the person does not necessarily have to do the *best possible* job, but does have to meet *acceptable standards* for the customer, client, or organization who is to benefit from the work. Very few companies or organizations, in fact, ever build the *best* product or provide the *best* service to the customer. They make a cost/benefit analysis and provide a product or a service that is deemed acceptable for the required standards. That doesn't mean that we necessarily build shoddy products. It simply means that we build a product that is "good enough." For example, the Mackinaw Bridge in northern Michigan is one strong bridge, decidedly stronger than a foot bridge over a stream in a country garden. The Mackinaw Bridge is stronger because it was designed to carry heavier loads and withstand more severe stress than a foot bridge. So when we design a foot bridge, we build it well enough; when we design the Mackinaw Bridge, it, too, is built well enough. Neither may be the best possible, and both vary considerably in structural standards, but each does an adequate job.

We also don't drive the finest automobiles that are made. We buy automobiles that will get us to and from work or across the country on vacation *relatively* trouble-free and in some modest degree of comfort, but which are less expensive to operate and drive than the very best. The automobiles we buy are "good enough."

Sometimes the Best Is Necessary

To be sure, sometimes the very best *is* necessary. If someone were concerned about painting the bottom of a sea-going vessel they would, no doubt, want to use the very best paint available, considering the abuse that the ship's bottom will be subjected to and the difficulty and expense of repainting. One may also be more concerned about the quality of an airplane engine than the engine of an automobile. As someone once explained, "You've never heard quiet until you've heard the engine in a single engine airplane quit running." Certainly, it seems more important for an airplane flying at 15,000 feet to have the very finest engine than it is for a car to have the same engine at ground zero. Indeed, at 15,000 feet—or 30,000 feet— it might be comforting to have two, three, four, or perhaps even more of the finest airplane engines that can be built. But the expense of this quality doesn't seem quite as necessary in a car.

The Problem with Perfectionism

The primary motivation for a boss to do the job rather than to assign or delegate the work to a subordinate is a result of the boss's inability to explain to others how to do something—or because the boss is a conceited, arrogant individual or an unreasonable perfectionist.

Perfectionism is a mental fetish that necessarily causes people to be resentful of unreasonable demands. Many people, when faced by unreasonable demands, often find it expedient simply to let the perfectionists do what they really want to do the way they want to do it.

Returning to the example of the child washing pots and pans, Sam may deliberately do a sloppy job, betting on the fact that Mom will find him impossible and unable to do the job right—and that good old Mom will go ahead and do the job herself. Sam, of course, learns this game very quickly. He also learns that it works not only when washing pots and pans, but also with other household chores—making a bed, cleaning a room, setting the dinner table, washing the windows, etc. Children are plenty smart enough to figure out that if they simply do not do the job *to the satisfaction* of the parent, the parent will end up doing it. In other words, they learn that one way to *upward delegate* work to the boss (Mom/Dad) is simply to do a half-way job. Then the perfectionistic parent will assume the work load and the child will get off scot-free without doing household chores.

This is not to suggest that as a parent or boss you should have to accept poor or sloppy work. But to get acceptable work done by a subordinate you must define meaningful performance standards and expectations and then see to it that the subordinate has ample tools, materials, machinery, training, and incentive. If the subordinate refuses to do a reasonable, *clearly defined* task, it can be interpreted as a refusal to do the job—but there certainly is no reason for the boss to feel that he or she has to do the job if it is to be "done right."

Other Problems with
Doing the Job Yourself to Get It "Done Right"

Anyone inclined to do all things to get them done "right" is not utilizing the talents of subordinates. He or she is also wasting time and probably not getting the job done any better. But there are some other, perhaps more important problems associated with the boss doing everything. For one, subordinates may be insulted at the suggestion that they really can't do the job acceptably well. When a boss says, "I'm the only one who can do the job 'right'," he or she implies that the subordinates are too dumb, lazy, irresponsible, inconsiderate, uncaring, unmotivated, or generally unworthy to perform satisfactorily. This can be offensive and can also create a real motivation problem. How many people are going to break their back to do a good, even adequate, job if the boss doesn't think they are capable of it? Most people have experienced this insult as a child. Inevitably some adult suggests that he or she should do the task at hand to be sure that the child doesn't somehow stink it up. The child usually gets miffed, and thinks that the adult is a meathead—and in many cases is justified in so thinking. But the child loses motivation to work well for the adult; and the adult, in turn, gets down on the child, thinking that "they're not making kids like they used to" and "the trouble with kids today is that they are lazy, unmotivated, inconsiderate, etc."

When Will They Learn How?
The Necessity of Training and Control

The bottom line to this problem is that the supervisor who is busy doing the job "right" does not have time to train and assign subordinates. Effective work assignment requires essentially two things: training and control. If a boss does not train a subordinate *how* to do a job, then the subordinate simply cannot do the job. But control is also imperative. While bosses *cannot* delegate or assign work to others if they are not trained, they *will not* delegate or assign work if there is no way to control or check up to see that the job is being done correctly.

If you want a job done right, train someone else to do it well enough—and then see that they do it.

This discussion points out that one basic truth, "If you want a job done right, do it yourself," is no truth at all. The only time when that idea holds up for effective managers or supervisors is when (a) the boss *can* do the job best, and (b) having the job done best is the *minimum* acceptable performance that can be tolerated for the job. Very seldom are both of these two requirements present, and in all other situations, there is only one truth to doing a job "right"—train someone else to do it right, and then behave like a real boss and devise some method to check and see that the subordinate is doing the job *acceptably* well.

3

Hard Work
Never Hurt Anyone

If "hard work never hurt anyone," how come "All work and no play makes Jack a dull boy"? Very few people would contest the notion that working hard contributes to success, but a lot of people who really work hard are never gigantically successful. So *is* there really a parallel? Perhaps success comes from *appropriately applied* hard work: "Work smarter, not harder," or "How soon we grow old, and how late we grow smart." Success actually depends on applying talent and effort in the appropriate direction at the right time. Diligent work efforts do *not* necessarily result in the attainment of success.

Why Hard Work Seems to Pay Off

Most of us have been told since we were kids that hard work pays off, and many of us have found it to be true. Very small children who learn to tie their own shoelaces receive praise from the parents. The youngster in early school years receives gold stars on perfect papers; the slightly older student receives praise from teachers—and perhaps monetary reward from parents—for each "A" grade received.

Young teens need some money and are admonished to "get a job." By babysitting, mowing lawns, and delivering newspapers, they begin to realize that hard work pays off. So the truism becomes reinforced: If one works hard, one will be rewarded. Furthermore, we learn that if we do a *good* job, then we will get extra rewards—perhaps not always cash, but often the even more valued "psychic income."

Where Does It All End?

So the self-reinforcing cycle of work hard, get rewarded, work hard, get rewarded seems a never-ending cycle. But, of course, the game gets more complicated. Perhaps as a high school or college student you were tempted to cut a few corners or even out-and-out cheat. Rather than writing your own term paper, it seemed a lot easier merely to copy one a friend or older sister wrote. Or maybe you chose to reward (monetarily) some-one else to write your paper, or you just didn't feel like studying so you copied someone else's test. Inevitably, if you continued this life of crime, sooner or later you got nailed by the teacher and then learned the meaning of "plagiarism" and "dishon-esty." When that happened, you learned that not only does it pay to work hard doing one's *own* work, but also that taking the easy, lazy approach often gets you into a lot of trouble.

To be sure, some people who work hard at a life of crime would argue that crime *does* pay if you don't get caught. But the bulk of our society doesn't want to participate in illegal, immoral, or unethical activities. For the most part, the igno-minious feeling of being arrested and convicted is an apt deter-rent to keep people from doing wrong.

It Doesn't End, but It Does Change

In all the chaos of growing up, somewhere, somehow, a con-fusion begins to emerge. "Just how is it," thinks the English literature major busily writing a speech for her boss, "that in college if someone had a paper or report or a speech written for them and were found out, they were called guilty of plagiarism; but if my boss, Ms. Big Deal, does it, it is considered good managerial practice. She delegates well. She uses her subor-dinates' time and talents as a competent executive should."

We know that ghost writers exist. We know that very few executives actually manufacture, service, or otherwise *physi-*

cally or *personally* get involved in the products their organizations provide to consumers. We know that executives are good managers. But executives who are getting work done through other people are certainly taking advantage of others' efforts, are they not?

So You're Off and Running

Let's take a little journey through the life of a newly appointed supervisor.

Friday, 4:45 P.M.:

"Gregg," says the Big Boss, "I trust you know that your production supervisor just turned in his notice."

"Yes, Mr. Big," says Gregg. "Who's going to be my new supervisor?"

"Gregg, I kind of thought maybe I'd like for you to take over the job. What do you think?"

"Well, I don't know. Never really thought about it. Do you think I could?"

"Sure," says Big Boss. "I know you can. Besides, we can give you a 10 percent pay increase."

"Wow! Boy, that'd sure be nice. Do you really think I could do it?"

"Gregg, I know you could do it," says the Big Boss. "What do you say?"

"Well, sure, if you think I can."

"I know you can. This is official. Monday morning, you're the new production supervisor."

Gregg goes home all excited at the news. He's going to be the new boss come Monday morning! He gets home and tells his wife, "Guess what! I just got promoted to supervisor—got a 10 percent pay increase, too!"

His wife, Rita, says, "Wow, let's go out and celebrate!" So they have a big weekend celebrating their good fortune. Hard work has paid off again.

After a wild weekend of celebrating over the promotion Gregg goes to bed on Sunday night with visions of sugar plums dancing in his head.

He wakes up about 3:15 in the morning, finding it impossible to sleep. He thinks, "This is my big day. I'm going to be the boss today." Come 5:25 A.M., Gregg can't stand it anymore. He gets up and runs around the room 26 times, but that doesn't help either. Furthermore, he's awakened Rita who's not all that excited about seeing the sun come up. Finally he decides to get dressed and head on down to the shop. Driving along, however, a problem emerges. He thinks, "What if they don't want me to be the boss?" Then he thinks, "That's silly, Big Boss said I would be the boss."

But the thought continues to haunt him: "Big Boss said I was going to be the supervisor, but what if the workers don't want me to be the supervisor? Will I be a leader if I don't have any followers?"

Fortunately about this time the *truth* emerges to save the day, as learned truths from Gregg's early upbringing come to his mind: "Hard work never hurt anyone," "Idle hands are the workshop of the Devil," "A good boss will never ask someone to do something the boss can't do himself." Now he knows that he has the wherewithal to be a successful manager.

"Why, I've worked right along with those guys for years," thinks Gregg, "and I know what it's like down there in the trenches working day after day. No one's going to tell me that I don't understand, because I do. I'm not going to be asking people to do things that I'm not willing to do myself, so I know I'll make it."

Finally Gregg arrives at work. And the workers begin to file in. "Morning, boss." "Hey, you're the new boss today, aren't you?" "Boy, Gregg, you'll be a good boss. You know what it's like working here."

Gregg hears it all but in the back of his mind he wonders, "Are they just testing me or are they really showing me some respect?" Somehow they get through the day. It's not so good. But it's not so bad, either. Driving home Gregg thinks, "The biggest problem I had is that I wasn't organized. I wasn't ready for the workers when they came to work. I've got to do a little planning, get things organized, be ready at the start of the day. I know what I'll do," thinks Gregg. "I'll go in a little earlier tomorrow and get things set up."

So the second day, Gregg goes in a half-hour early, makes his plan, gets set. Again the workers file in and give their morning greetings. Gregg returns the salutations, but is a little better prepared, making comments such as, "Good morning, Bill, how ya doing today? Listen, what I want you to get started on is..."and "Hi, Chris, how are you today? Fine day, isn't it? Listen, what I've got laid out for you to start on today is...."

And the day goes better—a good deal better. Driving home that night, Gregg says to himself, "Hey, that going in early

worked pretty well. I'm going to do that again tomorrow."
And thus Gregg gets into the habit of going in early and getting ready for the troops. Now, Gregg is settling into the sad-
dle of supervisory managerial practices. Rita's not too sure
about this new schedule, but she's also aware of the rewards
hard work has reaped in the past, so she adjusts.

After two or three weeks of going in a half-hour early, as
luck would have it, something turns sour at work. Problems
come up. Gregg gets his first good reprimand from *his* boss.
And at the end of the day, sitting in his car, waiting his turn to
get out of the parking lot, Gregg thinks, "What went wrong
today? I really didn't know what was happening. In fact,
come to think about it, I don't know if Bill finished that order
for the clinic today. I better go check on that." So Gregg turns
around in the parking lot, reparks his car, and heads back into
the shop. He checks on the clinic job and then happens to
think about tomorrow's orders. He also happens to think that
he better check on the status of the Central Packing order and
then thinks of a few other things to check on. Next thing he
knows, Gregg looks at his watch and discovers he's a half-
hour past due at home. "I better get home, quick," he thinks
and heads out the door.

Driving home, Gregg thinks, "You know, I'm glad I went
back in and checked up on things. Somehow I feel more comfortable about being able to really get things laid out right in
the morning before everybody gets to work. If that means
staying late a few minutes every night, so be it. I think I'm
going to make a practice of this. It gives me better supervisory
control."

And so the next day, things go well for Gregg, and he gets
into the habit of going in a little early to make the plan for the
day, staying a little late to debrief himself, check up on what's
going on, and generally oversee the status of operations. But
what else has Gregg done? For one thing he has extended his
work week by about 5 hours by going in a half-hour early and
staying a half-hour late 5 days a week. But then that's not so
bad; after all, they gave him a 10 percent pay increase when
they made him supervisor. And he only got a 5-hour work
increase. Mathematics would indicate that a 5-hour work increase is a 12½ percent work increase on a 40-hour week—
not too bad for getting a 10 percent pay increase. No wonder
people are tumbling all over themselves trying to get appointed to jobs of supervisors so they can make less money
per hour, but work more hours. Besides that, his increased
working hours haven't been all that popular at home. He's
usually gone by the time the kids get up and now that dinner

has to be later, there's not much time left for fun—anyway, he's too tired for other activities after putting in a 9-hour day.

Does Hard Work Really Pay Off?

Is Gregg's work really going to pay off? He's logging time, to be sure. And doubtless he will have the approval of the Big Boss. "Gregg sure is a hard worker. What he lacks in supervisory skills, he makes up for in long hours." But is he really working successfully, or is he simply working longer hours? Isn't Gregg actually performing his supervisory activities on his own time, leaving 40 hours free during normal work periods to get involved in what others are doing, and not doing what his job really calls for—supervising and planning?

Management Work
Doesn't Have To Be Done During Business Hours

Facts are, what has happened to Gregg is the same thing that happens to many young supervisors who have learned that "hard work never hurt anyone" and "working hard always pays off." Furthermore, he is getting good strokes from his superiors, earning "attaboys" every day. So the system is still rewarding, the system still works.

But is he getting ahead? Is he really being rewarded? Or is he only a victim of the system?

While You're At It

Experience shows that, as the young supervisor grows professionally, he or she also grows older. And at some point in time one begins to wonder whether those long, hard hours are worth it—particularly if, as one grows into the job, additional responsibilities are added to the work requirements.

Gregg at some point is apt to get hit with a *"while you're at it"*: "While you're at it, Gregg, would you mind checking on this, too?" or "While you're at it, could you look into this problem we've got with the Swearingin order?"

Invariably, jobs continue to grow, and anyone who always thinks that hard work pays off will be more than willing to embrace additional responsibilities. Their work load increases, and so does the stress both on and off the job. But what about their effectiveness? The smart boss will learn to get work done by subordinates.

Management Work Is Highly Transportable

One nice thing about supervisory and managerial work, so it's said, is that it doesn't necessarily have to be done at the office or shop. One of the first gifts the aspiring executive/ supervisor usually receives is a manager's tool kit.* The big advantage to having a manager's tool kit is that you can put your managerial work in it and drag it home. Thus, management work does not *require* that you necessarily go in early or stay late. This is very accommodating because then a manager might even participate in a car pool and save fuel.

By dragging supervisory and managerial work home, you can work in the comfort of your own space. This is particularly desirable because before and/or after dinner you can sit in your easy chair and do your supervisory work of planning, conceptualizing, getting things organized, etc. Or if you really want to be comfortable, you can spread it all over the dining room table—or even throw it all over the bed. Of course, the latter may create some additional stress if, during a bathroom break, Johnny comes in and jumps on the bed or Mary, under direct orders, clears and sets the table for dinner. But after a few learning experiences, everyone learns to stay away from the "grouch" and you are left in solitude to pursue the more important tasks at hand.

Managerial tool kits are especially valuable for taking work on commuter trains and airplanes. Indeed, management expert Cletus O. Von Rostfarben once described the difference between managers and doers as the amount of "wallpaper" they are surrounded with in their seats. Put simply, a pipefitter is

---

* The term "manager's tool kit" is the correct term to use to describe containers sometimes erroneously called briefcases, attache cases, valises, etc.

seldom seen welding pipe on an airplane; but managers are often seen doing management work. In fact, some managers make a specific point before they board the plane to get the seat beside them blocked so that no one will sit in it and they "can do some work." And because they know in their heart that everyone admires a "hard worker," it has the added advantage of allowing others to see how hard they are working to get ahead.

Managing vs. Doing

This is no sarcastic review of how aspiring young executives get ahead. Certainly, logging long hours will result in a certain degree of success. Unfortunately, it is highly probable that until you learn to work effectively on managerial, executive, and administrative-type tasks, you are not apt to be a real success. Simply devoting a large amount of attention to detail will not get additional productivity or cause a rise in an organization.

Understand that doing management work at home or on airplanes is not necessarily the *best* time for it to be done. A supervisor or manager should do exactly what the title implies: plan and see to it that *others* do the necessary work. Furthermore, if the supervisor is doing his or her job, there should be no need to "take home" work. Those who do, although they may be considered "hard workers" or excellent mechanics, are seldom the ones who get promoted to an *executive* position such as Vice President of Production. Ultimately, the ability to get work done *through other people* still emerges as the underlying requirement for success as an executive. That means *not doing* the actual production job, but having *someone else* do it and harnessing the talents of their efforts in a meaningful way so the total productivity of the organization is enhanced.

4

Idle Hands Are the Workshop of the Devil

It was probably your saintly grandmother who originally laid on you the truth that "Idle hands are the workshop of the Devil." Almost all societies have some such statement extolling the virtues of diligent work. Why? There seems to be a common belief among much of the world's population that "If you aren't working, you are probably sinning."

The Need To Stay Busy

People have a certain need to achieve, to stay busy. There have always been monuments to build, mountains to level, rivers to control, frontiers to be pushed back. For some reason we feel good when we are engaged in some kind of productive employment.

But if one is not busy at some kind of productive employment, does that necessarily mean that their idle hands get into trouble? Some evidence suggests the contrary. James A. Michener, in his book *Hawaii*, described the original Hawaiian people as neither especially productive nor evil. While these unproductive people, from time to time, engaged in tribal wars (among the original Hawaiians, for example), those wars were neither more frequent nor more bitter than the wars that have been fought by highly productive, *non-idlehanded* "developed" nations of the world.

Was Granny Wrong?

But Granny still said it. And you probably still believe it—particularly when you look at your currently unemployed, able-bodied 16-year-old offspring...Who eats like a horse?...Who wants to borrow the car?...And needs gas money?...And maybe a loan?

And what about those employees you have—why don't they work til quitting time? Why do they think, "If one comes in late, one should go home early?" Why is it that one employee runs the copy machine while another one stands there to watch him, waiting patiently for the first to finish so that the second can begin—and maybe to discuss what they did last weekend?

Many bosses would like to see productive activity consistent and constant, throughout the payroll day. Total commitment from all employees—right? After all, they get paid consistently for eight hours a day. Thank God Grandma didn't tell people that they were probably erring if they *did* work hard.

But does Grandma's logic apply to you? How would you feel if your boss were to catch you at your desk, with *absolutely* nothing to do? Would you admit it and reply, "That's right. In fact, I was thinking about running out and getting a beer. Want to go with me?" Or would you say, "I was just starting the estimates on the impact of the Jones job on our position," and think, "Whew, I'm sure glad I didn't delegate working up these estimates to someone else or I would have been caught with nothing to do."

Is much of *your* work done because of the horrifying fear that you might be caught with *nothing* to do? And does that keep you from effectively delegating and assigning work to your subordinates, work that should rightfully be done by them and that would rightfully free you up to sit at your desk, clasp your hands together, close your eyes, and *think* about your job and how to manage even better—or maybe even read a book on how to manage better?

The Need To Be Needed

All of us seem to have, Grandma notwithstanding, some need to be needed. We like to be involved: we like to belong.

Any teacher knows that getting the student involved will get more commitment and productivity. It's a trick of the trade. Even seminar leaders know that one way to get people to think they're getting a lot out of the seminar is to give them some kind of a paper and pencil exercise or group involvement exercise.

Many supervisors waste a lot of time because of their need to be needed. It's not unusual for the boss to be gone from the office for a half-day and call back two, three, or maybe even seven or eight times to find out how things are going and, in essence, find out if their wisdom, judgment, evaluation, or assessment is needed.

In fact, one of the great disappointments of those who do go on vacation and call the office is that they receive the good word that "everything's just fine." Even more disappointing is the discovery of the boss who returns after an extended vacation or illness to find that indeed things have "probably run better while you were gone than at any other time."

So insecure bosses who are trying to reinforce their need to be indispensable listen carefully for such phrases as, "Gee, Boss, I'm glad you called. What are we going to do about the shipment to San Francisco?" and "You've got to call Mary Snyder before 5:00 because she was really mad about that order and I didn't know what to tell her." Or even, "Boy, am I glad you called, Boss. I don't know whether to unplug the coffee pot or not. What do you think?"

The Desire for the Reward of Doing

If you are a manager and are disinclined to give up certain work tasks, you are feeding a very natural desire—the desire for the satisfaction and reward that inherently come from doing "doer" work but is not as inherently derived from managerial work.

"Doer" work is satisfying—this is why we often find hobbies and sports so rewarding. It is also the very reason that medical doctors advise patients who are experiencing stress to take up a hobby or a sport. Go jogging, collect stamps, build operating scale model locomotives, take up painting—those and many other avocations are suggested as ways to get away from the pressures of the office. The reason is because they are satisfying. If you paint a picture or run 6.2 miles, you've achieved something tangible. And that is a lot more satisfying than telling someone else to paint a picture for you or run 6.2 miles for you.

Put simply, "doer" work is always "gut-feeling" more rewarding, and management work is invariably less satisfying. Indeed, management work is only vicariously satisfying. Consider an example: Which would you rather do—hit the home run that wins the World Series, or be the manager of the team on which the player played who hit the home run that won the World Series?

All bosses *want* to believe that "Idle hands are the workshop of the Devil." But the emphasis on being busy focuses attention on "doer" work rather than on supervisory or managerial work. Obviously, a *good* manager is pleased to announce that the manager's players were the ones who won the World Series. But poor managers might not gain much satisfaction from that announcement. Psychologists tell us that most of us who *truly* achieve vicarious satisfaction do so primarily through the achievements of our children and relatively seldom through any others, including our workers.

Question: What Did You Do Today?
Answer: I Spent the Day Conniving

Thus, we've shown that part of the reason many bosses get more involved in doing "doer" work and fail to do their real job requirement—management work—is because there simply is not the *psychic reward* associated with the latter. Let's look at this from even another viewpoint.

Situation: You arrive home at the end of the day. You're exhausted and you show it. Your devoted lover takes one look at you and says, "Poor baby, you look awful. Can I fix you a drink?" Answer: "Yes, I'm beat."

"What did you do today that you're so tired?" asks devoted lover, handing you your drink.

"I spent the day conniving."

"You did what?"

"I spent the day conniving."

"You did *what?*"

"I spent the day conniving—you know, planning."
"You spent the day planning?"
"Yes, and I'm simply exhausted."
"You spent the day planning? What the hell are you planning? How the hell could you spend *all day* planning? Give me that drink. Fix your own drink. Why the hell are you tired if you spent the entire day planning?"

The foregoing situation is, of course, fictional—maybe. It probably has relatively little bearing upon the facts of life. No one would think that you would be deprived of "poor baby" time simply because you were exhausted from doing your *managerial* job of planning for the future. But what if the conversation went like this:

"Poor baby, you look exhausted. Here, let me fix you a drink."
'Yes, I'm beat. Simply worn out."
"How come you're so tired?"
"Two people didn't show up this morning and I had to help them unload one of the boxcars. Then, when that was done, I had to help them move the furniture out of my office to replace the carpeting. And then when I helped them pull up the carpeting, I even cut my finger. Look." (extending finger)
"Oh, you poor baby. Here, let me kiss it and make it better. Why don't you lie down and I'll fix your drink."

Obviously, the second story will merit retention of all "poor baby" rights. And if the cut finger is still bleeding, you may even merit a refill on the drink. But in the initial situation, you might be on shaky ground in retaining "poor baby" rights because, after all, how could you be exhausted if you merely spent the day planning, using your brain, doing managerial work?

The Need to Put Some of You in It

Yet another reason that many bosses get embroiled in doing things they shouldn't do, to the neglect of things they should do, is the inordinate need to put some of yourself in any job that is done; the need to "get your oar in the water"; the need for the "fine guiding hand" of the boss to be on the tiller.

It is not unusual in the Air Force to have the general ask the pilot if it would be alright for the general to "take over for a while." Everyone understands the need to keep one's hand in; but perhaps not everyone understands the intensity of that need. To develop this concept to its ultimate proportions, consider the following example.

How To Bake a Cake

As anyone who's ever baked a cake from a cake mix knows, the directions are simple: You buy the cake mix at the store, you empty the contents into a bowl, you add two cups of milk and *one* egg, you mix up the contents, you put it in the oven, and—behold—a cake!

Now some people are not mentally inquisitive enough to raise the question of why you add *one egg* to a cake mix. (It's obvious that you add the milk to provide liquid to adhere the mix into a batter.) The reason that *one egg* has to be added to a cake mix is probably because it must be against international law to manufacture and sell a cake mix that does not require one egg. For if that is *not* the reason, the only other possible reason is that some 30 or 40 years ago, when cake mixes were first introduced on the market, they didn't sell well because they only required adding water to the contents in the cake mix box from which the cake was made. And anybody knows that there is little substantive nutritional value in water. Therefore, if you made a cake from water, you certainly weren't getting much of a cake.

So what does this all lead up to? The problem was not that cake mix manufacturers did not know how to dehydrate milk and eggs when cake mixes were first introduced to the public. They could easily manufacture a cake that required half a dozen eggs and two cups of milk already in the formula and that simply needed the addition of water as a moisturizer to transform it into a cake batter. Unfortunately, the cake mix manufacturers discovered that by requiring *only* the addition of water they destroyed the value of the cake in the mind of the consumer. If they left *one egg* out (and the milk—need the moisture, you know), the cake mixes became much more acceptable to their customers. Then one *knew* that there was some *substantive nutritional value* in the cake and that, without doubt, the cake was going to taste better and be more wholesome.

The moral of the story is that most people have a need to contribute something of themselves to be involved. By being required to add an egg, you contribute more than you do just blending in water. It is all part and parcel of the "idle hands" problem for managers.

The upshot of the whole problem of Granny telling you "idle hands are the workshop of the devil" is that she was simply reiterating one of the most commonly believed truths of all the truths: Anything worthwhile takes some work, best of all backbreaking, hard work. But management experts know that the underlying compulsion to work (and the belief that if one works hard, one will get ahead) has little or no bearing on managerial success. What the compulsion does is cause bosses to stick their oar in the worker's pond, make waves for the worker, and waste time. It's far better advice to judiciously consider what work you should do, when to do it, and how to do it, rather than frenetically engaging in activity just for the sake of doing something.

III

Truth in Leadership

5

A Good Boss Will Never Ask Someone To Do Something the Boss Can't Do

The "truths" that exist about leadership are probably more nearly universal than many other truths. Just about everybody has had a boss at one time or another, just about everyone has developed some idea about what is and is not good leadership.

One of the more commonly heard truisms about leadership is that a "good" boss will never ask a subordinate to do something that the boss can't do. This stems from the old idea that if you haven't done it, you don't understand it. What's more, if you don't know how to do it and you are unknowing of the peculiar difficulties or unusual circumstances found in doing it, you really cannot boss it. Why? Because you plain don't know what is necessary.

Many are the troops, it is reported, who have had a high degree of respect for the leader who has been "down there in the trenches with us" and who "really understands." A good deal of this belief derives from the idea that "You don't know what it's like fighting alligators 'less'n you've spent some time in the gator pit."

Essentially, expressing the idea that you shouldn't ask someone to do something you can't do yourself is a way to put down leaders who aren't well liked. A statement such as "What does she know about bossing a word processing unit; she's never even used one of these typewriters," or "By God,

I'd like to see him do that. Why, I'll bet he couldn't last 30 minutes on this job. But he sure does like to tell you how you ought to do it," or "Ain't that new boss a dandy? Bet he's afraid to get his hands dirty" all serve as put-downs, attesting to the incompetence or unfitness of one's leaders.

But the "truth" of a good boss being "someone who has spent some time in the 'gator pit" not only has been propagated by *doers*; it has also been corroborated by them. "Ain't it so, Lefty?" "You bet, Shorty." But such ideas have *only* been propagated and corroborated by *doers*—not managers. Successful leaders know that it is ridiculous to suggest that someone has to be able to do a particular job before bossing it. Believing such an idea causes a boss to attempt to gain self-esteem in the eyes of those who are doing the work, but not in the eyes of those *for whom the work is being done*.

It's Patently Absurd

First, it's plainly absurd to never ask someone to do something you can't do yourself. Carried to its logical extreme, this could create a great deal of difficulty if you were in desperate need of open-heart or brain surgery (unless, of course, you are a surgeon). The same thing is true in even somewhat less than life-and-death oriented assistance. Suppose you need to fly from St. Louis to Dallas in a commercial airplane. Unless you are a licensed pilot, you'll have to ask someone else to fly the plane for you.

The facts are that we are totally dependent upon others and must every day ask people to do things for us that we can't do ourselves. Bringing it closer to the real world, consider your need for food. A very small percentage of our population really knows anything substantive about growing fruits and vegetables or raising cattle and poultry. Thus, most of us are totally dependent upon others to do the work necessary to stock our grocery stores and provide us with the foodstuffs we need for daily survival. The same thing is a reality in most of our daily activities—like asking someone to repair our television set, fix our plumbing, or pave our streets. Whenever we do those and many other things, we are still asking people to do things we really haven't done ourselves and probably can't do—at least not very well until we are trained and have some practice at it.

In fact, we often not only ask others to do things we can't do well ourselves, we pontifically demand that they do it correctly, even when we may or may not know what a correct or well done job even looks like *if we see it*. How many of you can truly pass judgment on whether or not your TV repair was done "right," or must you merely make the value judgment that "It works alright, so I guess it was correctly repaired."

The Little Piney River, Newburg, Missouri

I often recall an enlightening experience I had as a young man while working as a common laborer for the Missouri State Highway Maintenance Department. It seems that a bridge that crossed the Little Piney River at Newburg, Missouri was getting old and in disrepair. The specific problem with the bridge was that one of the pilings had not been poured on bedrock and had begun to settle; this caused a sag in the bridge which, if left uncorrected, would ultimately cause the bridge to fall down. In an effort to save the bridge, three common laborers (myself at 18 and two others who were around 30) were each issued one pick and shovel and told to dig a hole beside the existing piling so that a reinforcing piling could be poured to prevent the original from slipping further. This, of course, necessitated a good-sized hole: 8 feet wide by 6 feet deep, and perhaps 24 feet long.

Now, it was midsummer with temperatures pushing 100 degrees and humidity right behind. Nevertheless, the three aforementioned intrepid laborers persevered, flailing picks and manipulating shovels more or less on a consistent basis. Before long the foreman came driving up. Now as things were at that time in the world, foremen *always* wore a little uniform: dark pants; short-sleeved, white, polyester shirt; and a little tie. The foreman stumbled down from the road bed to the enlarging hole beneath the bridge, looked in at the three intrepid laborers, and suggested in a not overly friendly way that they really weren't getting much done and that he could probably have done more in less time than the sum total work of the three intrepid laborers.

The response of the IL (intrepid laborers), of course, was to work diligently and fervently at this point, with rocks, dirt and other extraneous matter literally flying from the hole.

Satisfied that the work pace had picked up somewhat, the foreman suggested that he was leaving, but that he would be back in a few minutes to see that the IL were really finally getting after it—and he drove off (in his air-conditioned pickup truck, fan belt squealing appropriately).

The IL immediately quit as soon as the foreman drove off. The reason: They were exhausted from the feverish activity of the past five minutes while being berated by the foreman. It was at that point that lightning struck, creating the great awakening of the mind. While leaning on my shovel, I was nudged by a fellow IL who said something to the effect of "By God, I'd like to see him get down here and do a day's work," nodding his head toward the departing foreman's truck. 'Yeah," said the other IL. "Boy, it's down here where you prove what you're really made of." My only thought was that those men really thought that the foreman ought to get down and prove that he could grub this stuff out as well as they could. It was somewhere about that point that I decided that I'd rather be a manager than a doer.

Management by Example

People involved in grunt work identify a good boss as one who has the ability to get in and grub along with grunt workers, to understand "first hand" what the work is all about. This is called *tribalistic behavior*. Tribalistic-type employees tend to view a good boss much like a tribal chieftain. They expect the boss to act like someone who understands their problems, hardships, and difficulties, and they react negatively to bosses who are not willing to give them a hand from time to time. They insist that a good boss "understands" what their problems are, including the problems of physically doing the work. They want a supervisor who will interact with them on a visceral or gut basis. Cerebral and mental boss/subordinate relationships are essentially rejected by the tribalistic person.*

Tribalistic types also tend to feel that a good boss is someone who should set a good example. Because of this fundamen-

---

* For academic treatment of this concept, see Clare W. Graves, "Levels of Existence: An Open Theory of Values," *Journal of Humanistic Psychology*, Vol. X, No. 2 (Fall 1970), pp. 131-155.

tal belief, many supervisors also feel that if they want someone else to do something, they need to set the example and prove that they're not "too good" to do it themselves. Therefore, we find bosses who won't take vacation time between Christmas and New Year's if they expect their employees to come in between Christmas and New Year's to take inventory. Or bosses who won't come in late or go home early—or if they do, they must carefully explain to their employees why they came in late or are leaving early. Or bosses who won't expect their employees to clean up the wash room unless they also take their turn cleaning up the wash room.

"Management by example" has popular acceptance among tribalistic-type employees and employers. But it generates a great deal of disdain from those who truly understand managerial behavior. Setting an example may make one a "good ole boy (or girl)," but it doesn't necessarily make one an effective supervisor. About all it effectively accomplishes is to raise the expectation of one's subordinates that the boss should take a turn "like everybody else" rather than managing to see that the *appropriate person* does it.

Employees really don't expect bosses to do their work. Frankly, they'd rather have the boss be a *good boss*—that is, do the planning, organizing, directing, and controlling necessary to make their job easier to do. For example, consider military service and that ever-detested job called KP. Of course, everybody in the service wants to eat (maybe they complain about the food, but they still want to eat), but nobody wants KP. The reason is because people have a biological need to eat, but not an instinctive love for washing pots and pans, peeling potatoes, and cleaning up garbage. So how do leaders in the military service get people to do KP? The answer is they get the employees (soldiers) to *want* to pull KP. How do you do that? Simply: You use a duty roster.

It's Got To Be Fair

What does a duty roster accomplish? It makes the situation fair. Everyone wants to eat, but no one wants to eat food that is going to make them sick. Therefore, everyone agrees that KP is necessary. They just don't want to have to do it themselves. Well, not even that, really—they don't want to have to do *more*

than anyone else does—because that's *not fair.* The military accomplishes fairness by having a duty roster. Every soldier
knows that, while he or she may have to pull KP tonight, everyone else in their squad will have to pull KP *before the first
soldier has to again.* No one will argue that's not fair, can they?

Sure they can, because it's not really fair at all. Why?
Because the officers never pull KP—just the troops. And if one
is worried about fair, that ain't fair. But the troops never complain because they don't *think* the officers are supposed to pull
KP. They are never told to expect the officers to pull KP and
officers *aren't supposed* to pull KP. The officers are supposed to
be planning the war (or at least staying out of the troops' hair).
Indeed, if the officers volunteered to pull KP, there might be
some serious repercussions. Some troops might raise questions
such as, ''If we make the officers pull KP, who's going to be
leading us?'' While in peacetime that may not seem to be such
a critical question, in wartime it becomes a major concern. And
in high-stress situations like war, it's not unusual for troops to
complain that maybe the officers (managers) really didn't have
enough time to evaluate the situation, plan strategies, and
implement them through the troops. ''Here, sir, let me wash
the dishes. You figure out how to get us out of here.''

We see very clearly, then, that there are many reasons why
the ''basic truth'' of not asking someone to do something you
can't do yourself is *totally unrealistic.* We have to ask others to
do things we can't do. It is simply a put-down toward a leader
by tribalistic-type employees who would like to raise their own
egos by default. Realistically, most subordinates really don't
want the supervisor/managers doing their work. Consider, for
example, what happens in craft union situations where a foreman picks up the tools and begins doing work that is within the
jurisdiction of the union members. The union may create a
''wobble''—that is, walk off the job because someone is taking
work they feel is theirs. Anyone experienced in labor relations
knows that is a very likely result because the foreman is
viewed as stealing the work of the workers—an intolerable
situation to any union loyalist.

The Flaw of Affiliation

This whole ''truth'' comes from our want to be well liked.
We all have a desire that David McClelland of Harvard Univer-

sity calls "the affiliative motive," some latent desire to be accepted, loved, needed, etc. There seems to be a dream that "If I show people that I'm no better than they are, they'll think I'm a good guy (gal) and they'll therefore think more highly of me."

David McClelland reports very clearly that such "good guy" activity may well make a bum boss. Affiliative-motivated (compared to power-motivated) bosses are extremely likely not only to fail in accomplishing their desired goal of being well-liked; they are also more likely to fail in achieving high levels of productivity from employees than the more power-oriented supervisors and managers.

"Can't Do" vs. "Won't Do"

Many supervisors who believe in the "don't ask someone to do something you can't do yourself" adage are very quick to agree that a good boss has to ask people to do things he or she *can't* do. That covers the brain surgery problem. (I can't do brain surgery. Therefore I'll have to ask a brain surgeon to do it.) What the saying really means is that good bosses should never ask someone to do something they *won't* do themselves. It makes a difference whether they perceive themselves to be above doing the job or, for some reason (discomfort, danger), *won't* do the job. You shouldn't (as boss) ask someone to do something you *wouldn't be willing to do yourself if it were your job.*

There might be some validity to this argument. If you are not willing to work in a hot, dirty environment, should you ask someone else to do so? Or, if you're not willing to work around toxic chemicals, should you ask someone else to work in that situation?

While there may be some argument that you shouldn't ask someone to work in hazardous or dangerous conditions, there isn't anything *necessarily* wrong with it. Some people may choose to work in extremely hazardous situations as an opportunity to get something they want (perhaps high pay) that they see no other way of obtaining. Perhaps they don't care about the potential risks. An example might be catching King crabs off the Alaskan shores. Most people are not aware how dangerous this is, and they might never purchase King crab if they really believed in not asking others to do something they wouldn't do themselves. To be sure, the work is extremely dangerous, but people do it because they want to make lots of money in a very short time.

When we talk about the propriety of a boss asking someone to do something the boss won't do, we're not talking about asking someone to do some foolish stunt like jump out of an airplane without a parachute. There are "dirty" jobs that are very valuable to us—so valuable that we offer enough money to motivate someone to do them. We don't object to asking people to explore for fossil fuels in extremely treacherous areas just because we won't do it ourselves. It is immaterial whether bosses would be willing to do the job themselves. We're talking about *leadership.* And we're talking about how to get someone to do the job that needs to be done. Management by example simply doesn't qualify as a necessary and logical leadership strategy.

6

Do Unto Others as You Would Have Others Do Unto You

One of the surefire "truths" of managerial lore is the Golden Rule: Do unto others as you would have others do unto you. This suggests that if managers treat others, primarily subordinates, the same way that they want to be treated in return, all human relations problems will disappear.

The Realities That Shape Managerial Style

But the Golden Rule simply doesn't work in any real sense for managers and executives—because managers and executives are different from nonmanagers and nonexecutives. They are more *ascendant oriented*, upward seeking, and success oriented. *Indifferent* people care less about getting ahead and successfully climbing the corporate or organizational ladder. They are not necessarily unsuccessful—indeed, they might be extremely happy and very successful by their own definitions—but they are not particularly successful in terms of the usual definition of success, which is the acquisition of money, power, position, and control over others. Furthermore, because of their personal values, indifferent types *expect* to be treated differently and *should* be treated differently.

A third group is the *ambivalent* person, someone who defines success differently from both the ascendant or the indifferent types. Ambivalent types have an enormous drive to be competent, but are not particularly concerned about success in the traditional terms. They, too, must be bossed differently than the ascendant and indifferent types, because they, too, *want* and *expect* to be treated differently.

Because of the basic and essential differences in these personality types, the manager who staunchly subscribes to the Golden Rule is not particulary well advised. To understand more completely, fill in Figure 6-1.

Assumptions About People

Typical managers, whether line supervisors or top executives, have been exposed so thoroughly to "current managerial theory" that they have become incapable of thinking about employees except in terms of the highest human dignity.

The following questionnaire assesses these tendencies. The typical score of the "average worker" is 38.5; the average score for managers is 41.5. This difference suggests that the average manager is more in favor of "nondirective," "participative," or "consultative" management.

Reason for Confused Behavior

Industrial humanism has been interpreted to mean that "*all* people have a higher order of needs," "one must find fulfillment on the job," and "one works because one has ego motives, security motives, curiosity, creativity, and the desire for new experiences." It is easy for managers to agree with such statements; they are noble, and noble statements are currently popular. Furthermore, because we would like to believe that all people possess attributes identified with the elite of our society, the successful person (who does possess such traits) *erroneously believes that others possess them*. Now, the job of successful people is to bring forth these hidden qualities in others through training and experience.

FIGURE 6–1 *Assumptions About People Questionnaire*

	Strongly disagree	Disagree	Agree	Strongly agree
1. Almost everyone could improve their job performance quite a bit if they really wanted to.	____	____	____	____
2. It is unrealistic to expect people to show the same enthusiasm for work as for their favorite leisure-time activities.	____	____	____	____
3. Even when encouraged by the boss, few people show the desire to improve themselves on the job.	____	____	____	____
4. If people are paid enough money, they are not likely to worry about such intangibles as status or individual recognition.	____	____	____	____
5. Typically, when people talk about wanting more responsible jobs, they really mean they want more money.	____	____	____	____
6. Being tough with people normally gets them to do what is expected.	____	____	____	____
7. It is difficult to get employees to assume responsibility because most people do not like to make decisions on their own.	____	____	____	____
8. The best way to get people to do work is to crack down on them once in a while.	____	____	____	____

	Strongly disagree	Disagree	Agree	Strongly agree
9. It weakens a boss's prestige whenever the boss has to admit to a subordinate that the subordinate has been right and the boss has been wrong.	___	___	___	___
10. The most effective supervisor is the one who gets the results management expects, regardless of the methods used in handling people.	___	___	___	___
11. It is too much to expect that people will try to do a good job unless they are prodded along by their boss.	___	___	___	___
12. The boss who expects employees to set their own standards for superior performance will probably find they do not set them very high.	___	___	___	___
13. If people do not use much imagination and ingenuity on the job, it is probably because few people have much of either attribute.	___	___	___	___
14. One difficulty in asking subordinates for ideas is that their perspective is too limited for their suggestions to be of much practical value.	___	___	___	___
15. It is only human nature for people to do as little work as they can get away with.	___	___	___	___

Scoring: Plus 4 = each "strongly disagree"; plus 3 = each "disagree"; plus 2 = each "agree"; and plus 1 = each "strongly agree."

Consequently, these "crusaders for industrial humanism" commit a fatal error and, therefore, support an indefensible position.

Executives accept the notion of participative management (and managerial trainers teach it) because *they all believe it.* But, the problem is not in their believing it or in the way they practice or teach it. The problem lies in their *proselytizing* others to accept their beliefs and in their attempts to force subordinates to live with them. In short, today's lower- and middle-level management trainees suffer from consultants', trainers', educators', or bosses' dictates that they must be participative managers *because the consultant, trainer, educator, or boss is, and because such practices have brought success for the consultant, trainer, educator, or boss.*

The Golden Rule further causes problems because it is valid only when the person being managed—the employee—has the *same outlook* toward work as the boss. Doing unto others as you would have others do unto you is *not* necessarily the rule that results in profitable management. Participative management may work if the manager supervises highly-motivated people, but if a subordinate has a different outlook toward working, the Golden Rule is inapplicable. It must be substituted with a far more workable rule, called the Rule of Human Realism: do unto others *as others would have done unto themselves.* In other words, manage employees for what they are, *not* for what we would have them be.

Rule of Human Realism

The Rule of Human Realism tells enlightened managers to look beyond themselves and the supervisory techniques that work with them, and to look instead at their employees as individuals to understand *their* work attitudes. The wise manager refuses to accept the popular notion that participative management is the magic formula for all employees just because it has been successful with some or because it is personally appealing.

Several writers have attempted to explain the managerial thinking expressed here. Robert Presthus, for example, set down some of the differences between managerial and subordinate attitudes toward work. These differences are summarized in the accompanying boxed material, but basically can be described as (1) the *ascendant* viewpoint (which represents the outlook of the *typical* manager); (2) the *indifferent* outlook (which represents the frame of reference of most rank-and-filers); and (3) the *ambivalent* attitude (which represents the outlook of many low-level managers and aspiring managers-to-be).

Differences in Work Attitudes

Ascendants

Identify closely with the company.
See failure as reflecting personal inadequacies.
Want feedback from superiors.
Engage in ritualistic behavior to conceal resentments.
Want power for its potential influence.
Tend to be procedure and rule oriented.
Place personal success above acceptance by
    coworkers.
Have high visibility drive.
Go down hard when they fail.

Indifferents

Withdraw from identification with the company.
Prefer not to compete for rewards.
Avoid ego involvement with the company.
Gravitate toward off-the-job satisfaction.
Reject those who strive for success and power.
Demand individual treatment and recognition.
Get upset by anything not routine.
Frequently depreciate the things they produce.
Seek immunity to discipline by joining unions and
    otherwise identifying with immediate work group.
Tend to have satisfactory interpersonal relations.
Usually adjust (slowly) to change.

Ambivalents

Are creative but anxious about the work.
Tend to rise to marginal positions and have limited
    career opportunities.
Cannot reject a promotion even if they do not want it.
Tend toward the neurotic.
Always want change from the status quo.
High intellectual interests but low interpersonal skills.
Subjective, withdrawn and introvertive, given to
    displays of anger and temper.
Make it a rule to resist rules and procedures.
Have idealistic and usually unrealistic career
    expectations.
Avoid psychological involvement with the company.
Tend to feel that success comes from luck and is a
    denial of talent, wisdom, or morality.
Usually are out-of-step in the company.
Reject fellow workers and what they view as com-
    promises accepted by them in their relationship
    to the company.
Become disturbed by the fact that they are successful
    (if they do get a promotion).
Tend to display a compulsive interest in the job in an
    effort to gain recognition.
Are poor decision makers.

The Ascendant Outlook

Most successful people have ascendant personalities. Ascendants continually strive for success and have high upward mobility. They identify closely with the company and the job, and have a morbid fear of failure, particularly personal failure. Ascendants are sensitive to their superiors' evaluation of their performance. They tend to vent emotions on inanimate objects, are rather ritualistic in their behavior (particularly in making efforts to conceal resentment against others), desire to be in powerful positions, are rule- and procedure-oriented, and have a high visibility drive.

Most important, from a managerial-style standpoint, ascendants do not take failure easily and tend to place personal success before group acceptance. They devote little effort to being popular and require compliance with company rules and regulations, even when unpopular. Ascendants want desperately to succeed, but fear failure deeply because they have no friends to commiserate with. Ascendants may be subjected to a variety of "I told you so" reprisals from colleagues alienated in the struggle for success.

The Indifferent Outlook

Indifferents tend to withdraw from company participation, not particularly wishing to be identified with the job or the company. They neither compete for rewards, nor are they interested in sharing either ownership or profits of the company. They tend to seek off-the-job satisfactions, and categorically reject the value system of success and power that the ascendant personality embraces.

Typically, indifferents want individual treatment and recognition, and only pay lip service to getting ahead. They reject the striving and self-discipline of the ascendant, do not expect to accomplish much and so do not try hard, and tend to fail (by ascendant standards). On the other hand, they tend not to feel particularly disappointed if they fail because they never really thought they could succeed anyhow. Indifferents jealously guard their own time and clearly differentiate between work time and personal time. They feel worried and threatened by anything on the job that is not routine, and, more significantly, tend to depreciate the things they produce.

Because of their strong affiliative drive, however, indifferent types tend to have sound interpersonal relationships with co-workers and, as a rule, will adjust to almost any working circumstances. Also, because of their interest in good relationships and their disinterest in competition, they offer no real threat or challenge to anyone.

Ascendants disdain the noncompetitive attitude of indifferents because the ascendants perceive indifferents as being lazy. Indifferents, however, do not react with antagonism, but may either view ascendants as "kooks" with an unremitting desire to work, or else fail to understand the ascendants' drive; indifferents do not deliberately refuse to cooperate with anyone.

The Ambivalent Outlook

Ambivalents are both creative and anxious about doing their job. They may generate ideas, but fear implementing them because of possible consequences. Ambivalent types usually rise only to marginal positions within the organization. They tend to have limited career opportunities because of general reluctance to fully commit themselves to the job at hand, particularly if it requires assuming responsibility.

When ambivalents find themselves in managerial positions—either by default or through seniority—they really aren't well prepared. As a result, they develop hot tempers and/or become subjective, withdrawn, or introverted.

Ambivalents resist rules of the organization and yet, at the same time, they dream of success. They become easily frustrated with their jobs, which increases their "psychological distance" from the company. Ambivalents can't help but feel that *real* success is more a result of having done something illegal, immoral, or unethical than having worked hard to get ahead. They believe they have worked as hard as anyone, so what other reason could there be?

Ambivalent types are almost always poor decision makers. Their unhappiness with their job and their performance causes them to win, at best, the antipathy of the indifferent and the disdain of the ascendant, who see the ambivalent as a snivelling wishful-thinker and day-dreamer who fails to perform.

Impact on the Organization

Most promotion decisions are based upon qualifications, prior job performance, and extrapolated job performance, so ascendants rise to the top of any organization. Figure 6–2 shows the distribution that might be expected of ascendants, ambivalents, and indifferents in a hierarchical structure of a small organization consisting of 20 people. The organization is headed by an ascendant, as is the entire second level of management.*

---

* The example is a sample only, and may not actually be the case in all circumstances. Ascendants usually rise to the top but, upon reaching any given level in the organization, may become ambivalent or indifferent. Also, most people are a mixture of the three types; rarely does the pure ascendant, indifferent, or ambivalent personality emerge.

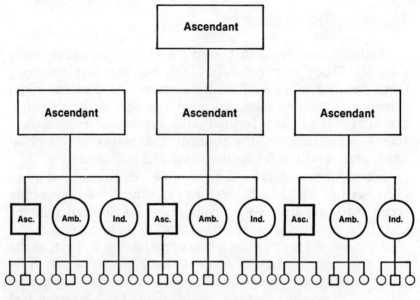

Key: □ = Ascendants
      ○ = Ambivalents and Indifferents

FIGURE 6-2   *Expected Distribution of Types of Employees*

Ascendants manage other ascendants, plus ambivalents
and indifferents. The lowest level in the organization is composed mostly of indifferent and ambivalent types (although
some "coming" ascendants are included in the group). Perhaps
25 percent of our population has a high power orientation and
tends to rise to higher positions in organizations.

Top Management—The Safety Zone

Top managers work in an ivory tower. Most of the people
who report to them are, or have been, ascendant oriented and,
therefore, could be managed in a participative, nondirective
fashion. The lowest level of management, the line supervisors,
have it tougher. Some of their workers show initiative, drive,
and creativity, but some *don't* and herein lies the difficulty.
While upper-middle and top-level managers manage
ascendant-oriented people—people who can be trusted to
follow their own lead and work toward organizational goals on
their own initiative—the percentage of indifferent and ambiva-

lent types is much larger in lower levels of the organization.

Lower-level managers who use participative techniques, including the Golden Rule ideas of treating subordinates as one would like oneself to be treated, have to be careful. Successful management at lower levels means applying the *right* style of supervision with the *right* subordinate in any given situation— not applying any "approved" style of supervision.

Top managers must also be aware of this and quit telling their junior executives to do unto others as you would have others do unto you. In fact, top managers may also need to reshape their thinking. Once it is recognized that there are different outlooks toward working—ascendants, indifferents, and ambivalents—and that people can change from one basic orientation to another no matter what their level in the organization, a pat managerial style simply cannot work. For example, an employee may be ascendant oriented and rise to a lofty position in an organization while still young and vital. Yet in later years, that same employee may develop an ambivalent or indifferent outlook toward work, even as a higher ranking executive. Therefore, the style of leadership which that person will best respond to at different times may change.

The Golden Rule may in fact do more harm than good in the area of training lower-level managers in leadership techniques, behavior, and strategy. The problem is that top-level management—the people who decide what kind of training should be given to lower- and middle-level managers—are themselves ascendant oriented and thus susceptible to management styles based on the Golden Rule. They make the grave error of embracing this idea and then end up *imposing* erroneous performance expectations on their subordinates.

Unfortunately, this expectation only increases managerial and supervisory headaches. It forces many lower- and middle-level managers to apply inappropriate tools of management that have been spawned and nurtured by well-intentioned but ill-informed soothsayers. This is not to say that *all* people dislike work, or that participative or consultative management is applicable in *all* cases, or that the Golden Rule *per se* is bad. However, as the Rule of Human Realism implies, understanding rational behavior and attitudes toward work is a far more profitable leadership style.

7

The Open-Door Policy

One sure-fire way for a manager to get unanimous agreement among employees is to suggest that "A fundamental principle of management is that of the open-door policy."

Unfortunately, the open-door policy, like many other "truths" about business, needs to be questioned a little more deeply. It may be a sound principle in many cases, but it is *not* necessarily appropriate in all situations.

What the Open-Door Policy Means

The open-door policy, of course, means that the boss should be available, accessible and approachable if and when a subordinate wants to have a talk.

Many corporations use what they call the open-door policy, but this really refers to the managerial communication process. This procedure states that "The boss's door is always open; anyone who needs to talk to a superior can do so, from first-line supervisor clear to the president or chairman of the board."

This latter open-door policy is not at question here. Many corporations who refer to their open-door policy mean this latter form whereby anyone can seek satisfaction of grievances by bumping as high up in the organization as seems to be warranted with legitimate questions or problems.

We could take to task this second form of the open-door policy, but usually the provision is stated that before someone can go in to see the president of the company, they must have talked to each level of supervisor along the way. In most organizations, employees can't simply walk off the assembly line and go in to see the president without working their way up the ladder and seeking satisfaction at lower levels.

The Care and Feeding of Monkeys

William Oncken and Donald Wass several years ago wrote a classic article in the *Harvard Business Review* entitled "Management Time: Who's Got the Monkey?"* They discussed the notion of monkey management, the care and feeding of monkeys, and, more specifically for our purposes, passing monkeys back and forth. The gist of their thesis was that when a subordinate goes to a boss with, "Hey, boss, got a minute?" the boss, operating from the open-door philosophy, is very inclined to say, "Sure, come on in, sit down. What's the problem?" At that point the subordinate says to the boss, "Golly, I've got this monkey on my back and I want you to take a look at it. It's really giving me quite a problem." The subordinate sets the monkey on the boss's desk for the boss to scrutinize. The boss looks carefully at the monkey, perhaps saying something to the effect of, "Gee, that certainly is an interesting looking monkey. I can understand your problem with it." Then the subordinate says, "Yeah, Boss, what are *we* going to do about it?" The boss, who isn't sure just exactly what to do about it, says something relatively safe such as, "Gosh, I don't know. Tell you what, let me think about that. I'll get back to you on it after lunch."

The subordinate at this point has successfully passed the monkey from his or her own back to the boss's back and simply replies, "Okay, I'll wait till I hear from you then." What the subordinate is really saying is, "Okay, and do a good job this time, you hear? I don't want you to stink it up like last time. I want some really good advice and input from you on how to do my job."

When a subordinate passes a monkey to the boss, he or she relegates the work back to the boss. And the boss, by accepting

---

* William Oncken, Jr. and Donald L. Wass, "Management Time: Who's Got the Monkey?" *Harvard Business Review* (Nov.–Dec. 1974), pp. 74–80.

the subordinate's problem, is really working for the subordinate, rather than vice versa. This is not the way it is supposed to be.

Can't You Handle It?

All bosses have to communicate to their subordinates, but many subordinates don't like to make decisions on their own. So, by taking advantage of the open-door policy, they essentially get the boss to do their job.

Now, if a subordinate is really not qualified to handle a particular problem, then the boss should be available to help. But if the subordinate should be able to handle the situation alone, there certainly is no reason to go in and hassle the boss. If subordinates can walk in with impunity, they can not only avoid doing their job, but also waste the time of the boss who will then have to do the job that the subordinate should have done in the first place.

The Revolving Door

Perhaps modifying the open-door policy is the solution; perhaps the "revolving-door" policy is more practical.

In a revolving-door policy, a boss, when approached by a subordinate who obviously is wanting to pass a monkey to the boss's back, says to that subordinate, "That's exactly one of the things I think you should be able to handle yourself. Why don't you go back and work on that, collect whatever information you need, and use your best judgment to make a decision. Certainly if you are as intelligent as I think you are and knowledgeable about your job, I'll back you up in any reasonable decision you make."

Don't Bring Me Problems, Bring Me Solutions

Many executives are already aware of the monkey-passing problem that results from an open-door policy. For that reason, a new philosophy has evolved, as exemplified by the statement, "I tell my employees not to bring me problems, but to bring me solutions." Unfortunately, bringing the boss *solutions* is only ever so slightly better than bringing the boss *prob-*

lems, and falls far short of the mark of having subordinates do the job they were hired to do.

If a subordinate brings the boss alternative solutions to a problem for the boss to make a decision, the boss is *still doing the subordinate's job*. After all, if the boss says, "Do alternative B, rather than A or C," he or she is *deciding* for the subordinate what is to be done. In so doing, the boss has relieved the subordinate of the responsibility for making the decision. If the solution doesn't work, the subordinate will say, "Well, I did it the way you told me, solution B, and it sure didn't work. What do *you* want me to do now?" The implication, of course, is that it was the boss's decision and the subordinate was only doing what the boss said to do.

The Passing Fencepost

Any way you want to slice it, being readily accessible and available to a subordinate is apt to lead to upward delegation; that is, the boss gets to do the job that the subordinate is supposed to do. The boss is treated as a target of opportunity and gets dumped on in the process.

To show how this works, consider the example of someone traveling across the country with a male dog in the car. Sooner or later the car stops and the dog gets out. Any self-respecting male dog, immediately let loose from a car in the countryside, does one thing—hose down the first fencepost he can find.

Now why did the dog dump on *that* particular fencepost? Did the dog have anything *against* that fencepost? The answer is no. The dog picked *that* particular fencepost simply "because it was there." Nothing personal, you understand, you're just the first fencepost I saw.

In essence, employees do that with bosses, and often start by making statements like, "Hey, boss, got a minute?" It might be wise to say, "No, I really don't have a minute. Could I see you after lunch?" At least the audience would have to withstand the test of time.

All bosses have had to postpone talking with subordinates because the time was not convenient when they asked for a conference. When the boss looks up a subordinate later and asks what the problem is, the subordinate *can't remember* and/or replies, "Oh, since you were so busy, I asked Harry and

Harry told me to..." or "Oh, never mind, I figured it out myself." Probably 50 percent of the time when a subordinate asks a boss for a few minutes, the boss is simply being made a target of opportunity, and the subordinate is simply finding it easier to ask the boss rather than go ahead and do his or her own job.

When Does Someone
Need an Appointment to See You?

Some bosses are big deals. Some bosses are simply jerks. But all bosses should have some amount of dignity and respect, which can in part be realized by successfully operating a revolving-door policy.

If you are a first-line supervisor, your subordinates do not need to make an appointment to talk to you. Just how big a deal must you be before you can operate as a professional executive? Must you be president of a giant corporation before you have a secretary to schedule appointments?

Consider the small sporting goods chain in Canada, which is now defunct, and which may have become defunct because of the owner's nonexecutive posture. The open-door policy of this company did not in itself cause the company's bankruptcy, but it probably contributed handsomely.

This particular executive's office was the first door that anyone passed after entering the reception area. That made the owner a target of opportunity for anyone who entered, be it a sales representative, a bill collector, or a Girl Scout selling cookies. *Anyone* who wanted to simply drop in the owner's office could do so at any time by simply poking his head in the front door and saying, "Hey, got a minute?"

The accompanying drawing shows how this type of office arrangement makes it very easy for anyone to get to the owner's office. In a real executive setting, executives are cloistered, removed from easy accessibility of any Tom, Dick, or Mary who wants to go in and give the boss "an earful" or "relegate" some work to the boss.

One vivid description of this can be found in John Z. DeLorean's book, *On a Clear Day You Can See General Motors,* where he describes the meaning of the fourteenth floor of the Fisher Building in Detroit. You don't just stumble into the

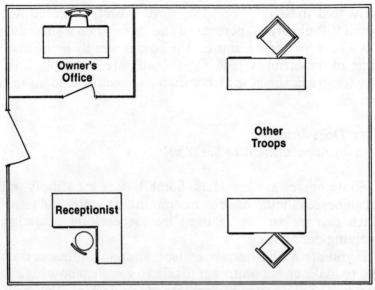

FIGURE 7-1

"Head Shed" and walk up to the throne without an appointment. You don't do it at General Motors *and you don't do it at any well-run business.*

Managers should avoid simply setting up barricades between themselves and all subordinates. But they should also understand the fallacies of the open-door policy and how relegation not only consumes time, but also makes employees dependent upon the boss while at the same time forcing the boss to do the subordinate's job. Bosses should never be aloof or arrogant and totally inaccessible to employees. But they should not do a subordinate's job either. It's poor management.

8

Nice Guys Finish Last

The immortal words of Leo Durocher are hard for us to accept. Many refuse to believe it. They still believe in the Golden Rule and the importance of being well-mannered, discreet, and, to put it bluntly, not the south end of a north-bound horse.

But there are many people who agree that nice guys *do* finish last. Most bosses are competitive, aggressive ascendant types who see failure as a reflection of personal inadequacies, who want power for its potential influence, who place personal success above acceptance by fellow workers, who have high visibility drives, and who go down hard when they fail.

Is It True That Nice Guys Finish Last?

It is, alas, probably true that nice guys finish last. One example is in the study of negotiations. Researchers agree that those who negotiate tough simply get more, whether they are contract negotiations between two corporations, negotiations between a buyer and seller of real estate, a labor contract negotiation, or even a boss and a subordinate negotiating a pay raise. The following list is typical of negotiation skills.

1. Use surprise.
2. Never go tit for tat; a *quid pro quo* is bad form.
3. Always bargain or negotiate on a piece-meal basis.
4. Close in a crunch.
5. Never list or itemize what you're willing to give the adversary.

6. Make yourself unavailable for contact by your adversary, as by leaving town on business.
7. Study your adversary's demand pattern and learn to anticipate when they're weakest.
8. Study your adversary's needs and bore in on those.
9. Give a *little* occasionally, but not too often.
10. Use the team approach and have plenty of yes men with you.
11. Get your adversary's leader called from the room and pick away at the remaining minions.
12. Always encroach on the adversary's territory.
13. Use time pressure and deadlines to your advantage, but be cavalier about your adversary's time pressures and deadlines.

This is what any negotiator does who wants to *win*. It's not very nice, but remember, those on the other side are probably playing by the same set of rules. This means if you "play fair" you're operating at a disadvantage before you even begin.

But Isn't a Win-Win Solution Best?

Most people engaged in conflict resolution tell of three basic attitudes assumed in a conflict situation. One is "I'm going to win, but you're going to win, too." Another is "I'm going to win, but you're going to lose." This, of course, is the most common attitude of antagonists in a conflict situation. The third attitude is "I'm going to lose, but you're going to lose, too."

I'm Going to Win, and You Can Do Anything You Can Figure Out to Do

We all agree on the advantages of a win-win attitude and on the unpleasant aspects of a lose-lose attitude. We all understand why two adversaries who play from an "I'm going to win and you're going to lose" attitude will not come off nearly as nice as two adversaries playing by the win-win rules. Yet, in truth, we seldom actually play with a win-win attitude. Most of us play with the idea that win-win is best and would be ideal, *but whether or not you win, I am going to win.* This attitude boils down to "I'm going to win and you can do anything you can figure out to do."

Alan C. Filley* and Larry L. Cummings** cite statistics about whether or not nice guys finish last in conflict resolution. In the vast majority of cases, the person who comes off resolving conflict as a win–lose battler always beats those who compete on a "friendly helper" basis or a lose–lose basis. They also win out over the win–win problem solver and the compromiser.

Philosophical Beliefs Necessary
for Win-Win Attitudes to Work

Why are people who enter adversary relationships as nice guys apt to lose?

If both adversaries play by the win–win rules, a win–win solution will probably emerge. But if *one* adversary elects *not* to play by those rules, then the same solution cannot work. For this reason, one must play conflict situations from the *lowest common denominator*, not from the highest common denominator.

Think of a street fight. You might try to defend yourself by subscribing to the Marquis of Queensbury's rules of boxing. But if your adversary pulls a knife, hits below the belt, and otherwise disregards all the Marquis' rules while you stick to them, someone is likely to get killed—and it won't be the one breaking the rules. The one who gets killed is the one who says, "Sir, don't you see, that's not a fair way to fight."

Conflict resolution demands certain conditions in order to work in a problem-solving way, including:

1. A belief by both parties in the *availability* of a mutually acceptable solution.

---

* Alan C. Filley, *Interpersonal Conflict Resolution* (Glenview, Ill.: Scott, Foresman and Co.), 1975.

** L.L. Cummings, D.L. Harnett, and O.J. Stevens, "Risk, Fate Conciliation and Trust: An International Study of Attitudinal Differences Among Executives," *Academy of Management Journal*, Vol. 14 (1971), pp. 285–304.

2. A belief by both adversaries in the *desirability* of a mutually acceptable solution.
3. A belief by both adversaries in the desirability of cooperation rather than competition.
4. A belief by both adversaries that each is of equal value and what each one wants is important.
5. A belief that the other one is making a legitimate, honest statement of how he/she feels about the situation and what he/she wants.
6. A belief by both adversaries that "expressing" their differences of opinion honestly and openly is helpful and will lead to the resolution of their differences of opinion.
7. A belief by both adversaries that the other one is trustworthy and is telling the truth and/or otherwise legitimately presenting how he/she feels.
8. A belief by both adversaries that the other one *can* compete but chooses to cooperate and *is* cooperating.
9. A belief by both adversaries that the other one is competent and is capable of doing his or her job satisfactorily.
10. A belief by both that any information that they have should be shared with their adversary openly and honestly.

These beliefs will lead to cooperation and the ultimate resolution of conflict on a win–win basis. Unfortunately, it's naive to think that adversaries will subscribe to all ten beliefs: twenty out of twenty is virtually impossible to pull off.

The Advantages to the Russian Method of Negotiating

Two types of negotiation strategies predominate. One, called the *Russian method* or the *competitive tactic*, is when the player plays to win in order to force the other side to lose. With this strategy, you can win as high as 90 percent of the time. (The other method, the *collaborative style*, is the win–win alternative suggested above.) The Russian method wins more, which ensures that nice guys do finish last. It employs some of the following techniques, none of which are "nice guy" strategies. They include:

1. Starting with tough, excessive demands, and insisting on getting more than any reasonable person would expect to get.

2. Not having the authority present at the negotiating table. The representatives who *are* at the negotiating table have little or no authority to actually negotiate anything. They therefore can make *demands to get* things, but cannot *approve giving* anything.

3. Using highly emotional negotiation strategies. A classic of this was Nikita Khrushchev at the United Nations taking off his shoes and pounding on the table in front of him, terrifying half the diplomats who didn't quite know what to do.

4. Taking the attitude that when an adversary makes any kind of concession, it shows a weakness and sets them up so you can take more.

5. Seldom, if ever, giving any concessions of any significance. Keep pecking away, trying always to get a little more, while at the same time being very reluctant to give any concessions at all.

6. Having a great deal of patience and a willingness to ignore deadlines intended to force issues, a situation that cannot be tolerated by anyone who respects deadlines. The not-too-well initiated person, facing this flouting of time pressure, may be stampeded into doing something ill-advised under the belief that the crazy fool they are negotiating with is simply willing to let everything go down the drain unless they make yet further concessions, thereby losing even more.

W.S.O.B.S.A.N.G.F.I.A.S.B.

A recently published book called *Why SOBs Succeed and Nice Guys Fail in a Small Business** owes its popularity to its ham-fisted, hard-nosed approach to leadership. The SOB book flies squarely in the face of much theoretical literature concerning participative management by showing supervisors that if they play to win they're more apt to win than if they play to tie.

---

* Anonymous, *Why SOBs Succeed and Nice Guys Fail in a Small Business* (Phoenix, Arizona: Financial Management Associates, Inc. 1976).

"Show me a good loser and I'll show you a loser" is becoming a popular sentiment in business. If you want to be a realist in the world of business, recognize that even "nice guy management" in an appropriate style doesn't usually work. Very simply, statistics show that nice guys *do* finish last when they play against a win–lose strategist in business.

Summary

Surprise! It's true. *Nice guys finish last.* We would all like to live in a world where nice guys end up on top, but the reality is, there just aren't enough nice guys out there to make those rules work.

Appendix to Chapter 8

Everybody out in the Parking Lot

One of the more dramatic SOB-type stories, which also happens to be true, serves to underscore why people who are aggressive tend to succeed in business far more than those who are not.

The story concerns Mr. Allen, owner and president of Magnum, Inc., located in Midvail, Missouri.* A few years after acquiring control of the company, Mr. Allen was disappointed that it was not producing as effectively as he had hoped. Furthermore, he was plagued by the nagging concern that he didn't know who was doing what and/or whether or not what they were doing was necessary. Also, he was having difficulty trying to get any definite answers as to what needed to be done and what did not need to be done.

One day, Mr. Allen decided that something had to be done—something drastic—something that would not be too popular. So he ordered everybody—*everybody*, even the telephone operators—into the parking lot.

---

* Names and places are fictitious.

You're All Fired

Once Mr. Allen had assembled all of his employees, he announced: "You are all fired. Repeat, all fired."

Naturally the workers were stunned in disbelief. What kind of a madman was this? How could he possibly fire everybody? The phone's ringing. Who's going to answer the phone? We've got products to ship. Invoices need to be sent out. We've got shipments to make. What's he doing?

The long and short of the whole experience was that he fired some 200 employees and told them that, while he would obviously have to rehire some of them, he was only going to rehire those that he needed when he needed them. And then he would rehire them one at a time. Naturally, as one would imagine, some 15 or 20 people were hired back the first day. The phone was ringing. And invoices had to be sent out. And products had to be shipped. But he didn't hire back very many the first day.

On ensuing days he hired people back as he needed them. But out of the 200 employees, he hired back fewer than 100. But the company began to make money, and operations proceeded smoothly. Some people who were not rehired didn't like Mr. Allen. But those he did hire back didn't think it was such a bad way to run a business.

On August 3, 1981, the Professional Air Traffic Controllers Organization decided to go on strike against the U.S. government. President Ronald Reagan announced that the participants in the (alleged illegal at the time of this writing) strike had 48 hours to decide to go back to work, or would be considered to have terminated their jobs. Approximately 12,000 of the 17,000 or so PATCO members did not go back to work—and what happened? The government has quit writing a lot of paychecks. Ultimately, some of those controllers have or will be replaced, but because the airlines also took the opportunity to cut back on unprofitable flights, it is doubtful that all 12,000 will be replaced for a good many years. In the meantime, the government is cutting expenses. Drastic action sometimes works very effectively.

9

A Good Boss
Is a Good Human Relator

A long standing favorite phrase of any manager is "human relations." Anyone who is good at human relations will doubtless be an effective leader. How can you argue with that?

What Is Good Human Relations?

Despite the prevalence of those who swear by the necessity of "good human relations," few can actually define it. Being a good human relator might mean that you are a nice guy. On the other hand, it might mean that you stand up for individual and personal rights. Or it might mean you are highly politic, or that you know how to sell. Yet again it could mean that you know how to say "no" tactfully or diplomatically. But being good at it ensures managerial success. Amen.

The History of Management Thought

Human relations, as it applies to business management, grew out of the 1920s and 1930s research studies conducted into employee productivity. Elton Mayo* might well be

---

* F.J. Roethlisberger and William J. Dickson, *Management and the Worker* (Cambridge, Mass.: Harvard University Press), 1965.

credited with launching the human relations movement as a
result of his research at the Hawthorne Works of the Western
Electric Company.

Mayo conducted experiments to gather efficiency-expert
data—time and motion study, right tool for the right job, etc.
One of his experiments came to be known as the "classic
lighting experiment," wherein he tried to determine the
optimal level of lighting for a production unit. The situation
involved a group of employees who were assembling relay test
switches and who needed to see what they were doing to be
sure that the work was done right. The big question was: How
much light in the work area was necessary and yet economical
for them to perform their jobs?

Isolating the Independent Variable

Research relating to human behavior requires both a test
group and a control group. The control group continues to do
everything the same old way it has always been done; the test
group does everything essentially the same way it has always
been done with one exception—the independent variable being
tested.

In the Hawthorne studies, a control group and a test group
continued working. For several days the intensity of lighting in
the test group was increased and the impact on productivity
recorded. Increased lighting clearly resulted in improved productivity. Yet after several days of increasing lighting intensity,
it became a matter of concern that they had reached the point
of diminishing returns of productivity, yet were increasing the
costs of the electricity.

The Problem with Diminishing Returns

In this case, a greater return (work productivity) was possible by increasing the independent variable (the lighting) but
the increased costs of the lighting may not be compensated for
with *enough* increase in productivity. Mayo was trying to find
the *optimal* level of lighting, not the *maximum* level of
lighting. Figure 9–1 illustrates his findings. As the level of intensity of lighting was increased, productivity increased. But
at some point productivity reached its maximum, irrespective

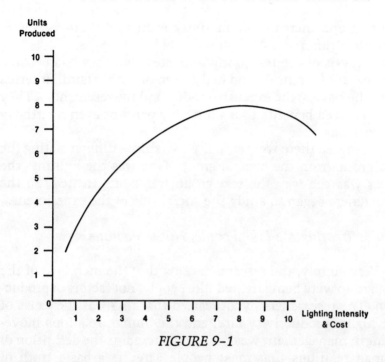

FIGURE 9-1

of the intensity of the lighting. Continued increases in the intensity of the lighting would only result in wasting electricity; it would not increase productivity.

Aware of this problem, Mayo *decreased* the lighting to find where the level of productivity would significantly *fall off*. He hoped to ascertain the *optimal* level of lighting—the point where most production was realized with least lighting.

Surprisingly, when they began to dim the lights productivity went *up*, not down. The next day they dimmed the lights again and, as on the preceding day, productivity went up again! You can imagine what such results do to a researcher! The theory was not proving out. One mission became overpowering: Get Productivity Down! They continued to dim the lights but for a while productivity continued to increase. When productivity began to decline, they were never able to get it as low as it was at the start of the experiment.

So Back to the Drawing Boards

What had gone wrong with the experiment? How could they increase lighting and increase productivity, then decrease lighting and increase productivity even more? Surely something was different. What could it be?

Analysis of the test group indicated that they had become the center of attention and had gotten on rather familiar terms with the bosses, the executive cadre, and the researchers. They also received benefits like a birthday party or even a birthday off with pay.

It seemed there were actually two things differentiating the test group from the control group. One was the lighting; the other was the way the test group was being treated. So the researchers began to study the social side of the experiment.

You're Treating Me Like People, Not a Machine

Very simply, the researchers saw that the members of the test group were being treated like people, not factors of production. The researchers hypothesized that this was the cause of the higher productivity rate, and the human relations movement in management was born. This remains the definition of human relations that most people agree is a basic truth of leadership.

What's Wrong with Good Human Relations?

As a result of the Mayo experiments, the 1930s and 1940s saw the expansion of the human relations movement in management. Experiments seemed to show that if a boss became a good human relator, he or she would necessarily realize better productivity from employees.

Fundamentally there are three things wrong with human relations: First, most bosses are not good human relators. Second, human relations is extremely expensive and isn't worth the cost. Third, some people don't like being human-related with, and thus the desired impact is not realized. Let's look at each problem closer up.

Some Bosses Aren't Good Human Relators

The average boss really doesn't get good marks as a human relator. It would mean that the boss would have to take a *genu-*

ine, sincere interest in the employees that he or she is supervising. But often that just isn't the case. Practically always when supervisors take a *"genuine, sincere* interest" in their employees, they're doing so to increase productivity. Their primary scheme is *not* to take an interest in people. Therefore, many bosses *feign* interest in people in an effort to trick them into increased productivity. This transparency is practically always caught.

Most bosses don't come to work and ask a subordinate how they are. Statements such as, "Hi, how are you? How do you feel? Are you comfortable? Can I get you your pipe and slippers? How about a cup of coffee? Can I set the air conditioner a little cooler for you?" just don't happen very often. Practically always when the boss says "Good morning" to an employee it's followed with, "Did you get that project finished?" or, "You know we've got to get the Jones job finished before noon," or, "Where did you put the report on the Southwest District?" They're not inquiring about whether or not an employee is happy; they are inquiring about whether or not the employee is being productive. They want to know how things are going—productivity—performance—shipping schedules— *are customers happy?* Most employees don't feel that their bosses are good human relators because they're not. They're more interested in productivity.

We Really Can't Afford Human Relations

Human relations is also very expensive. It was one thing for Elton Mayo to give a birthday party for the members of his test group. It was something else to give them their birthdays off with pay. It was yet another thing to have spawned the entire fringe benefits program in our society today.

Most employees say they'll work harder if the boss treats them like real people, recognizes that they have birthdays, need paid holidays, etc. But the truth of the phenomenon known as the "New Fur Coat Syndrome" destroys the efficiency of this belief.

The first time the boss sends an employee a birthday card the employee may be motivated by thinking the boss likes him and treats him like a person. But when he finds out the boss didn't really send the birthday card (the boss's secretary did), he begins to wonder about the genuineness of it. And he begins to think the boss is cheating. Furthermore, he finds out that the boss doesn't even know it's his birthday, or even care—that the boss simply has set up a *system* to procedurally and mechanically human relate with him. So he begins to take sanctuary in the idea that he really shouldn't have to offer his *quid pro quo* for the fringe benefit, because the boss is trying to trick him into working harder. So he doesn't work any harder. But he doesn't *not* take the fringe benefit. He just doesn't work any harder. In fact, he might even work slower because he resents being tricked.

Fringe benefits in the short term may motivate people—until the trick is found out. In the long run, insincere human relations efforts don't motivate people to work better. "So what else have you done for me today?" becomes the question. The "New Fur Coat Syndrome" rides again. "So you gave me a new fur coat yesterday. So what? I was nice to you yesterday. What are you going to give me today?"

Statistics show that fringe benefits have risen to a dramatic 50 percent of payroll in the United States. But anyone can read in the newspaper that productivity has certainly not increased by 50 percent. Even those who are extraordinarily labor sympathetic will not suggest that productivity has increased here (or anywhere else in the world) by that amount. The facts are that fringe benefits have been used to try to trick employees into wanting to work harder. But the trick has backfired! The cost is incurred, but the productivity has not been realized.

Some People Don't Like Being Human-Related With

The third thing that's wrong with human relations is that a lot of people don't like being human-related with. I am reminded of an experience on my first job as a management trainee in a grocery chain.

While training to be a store manager, I was told that "A good trick of the trade is, when you come to work every morning, go around and seek out the employees in the store and say 'Good morning' to them and otherwise let them know that you are glad they are in the store."

This, of course, sounded like good stuff. After all, I was newly graduated from a reputable business school where I had read good books on human relations as it was taught in the mid-1950s. This guy obviously had read the same stuff and knew the latest, up-to-date management techniques.

However, as part of my training, I was required to work in the store along with all employees in order to get the "hang" of the business. By working shoulder to shoulder with the employees of the store, I got to know many fellow employees very well. After a while they no longer looked at me as a management trainee, but rather as a fellow worker. Then one day as the store manager was making his daily trek around the store and saying "Good morning. How are you?" to everyone, one employee said to me, "I can't stand the store manager coming around every morning and saying 'Good morning.' So you know what I do? I hide from him all morning so that when he finds me he has to say 'Good afternoon.'"

The moral of the story is that people begin to realize when the boss is playing the old no-brainer game of being friendly, the purpose of which is to psychologically trick the employee into working harder.

The Era of Manipulation

The problem is clear: Most bosses who try to be good human relators do so to increase productivity. They feign interest in employees, and therefore become psychological manipulators. To put it frankly, they feel that blowing in the employee's ear will get the employee to knock herself out trying to work harder because of the nice things that were said by the boss about the employee's productivity. But this thin veneer is seen through early in the game and a great deal of resentment is built up toward it.

But There Really Isn't Anything Wrong with Good Human Relations

The truth is there really isn't anything wrong with *good* human relations. Bosses who do take a genuine, sincere interest in their employees and relate well with them will find that their employees do work better for them. But if the boss relates interest in a connived, maliciously aforethought practice, the scam will be seen through for what it is and will be rejected by the employees.

We still have basic evidence that good human relations will work. But we do *not* have any evidence that *manipulative* human relations will work. Thus, anyone who believes that a good boss is a good human relator is not necessarily wrong. Nor are those people believing in an untruth unless they think, in addition to the good human relations, they don't really have to be sincere, just go through the motions. So maybe good human relations is alright. The question is: Do you really mean it if you think you are practicing it? Are you really interested in doing it *not* for the sake of increased productivity but simply because you're *interested* in your employees? If the answer is yes, then good human relations is a workable managerial truth.

IV

Truth in Managing Others

10

To Do Something Right
Takes Time

There's a long list of clichés dealing with the management of other people's time. One, of course, is that if something is to be done right, it is going to take some time to do it: "All good things will come in due time." "A watched pot never boils." "You can't hurry something of value."

Origins of the "Right Takes Time" Myth

Whenever we're required to wait, we presumably savor the results of the waiting all the more. Patience builds character. We've all heard this as a child. Who couldn't wait for the pie to cool, or for Santa Claus to arrive, or for Mary's birthday party on Saturday morning? We teach our children this myth and we perpetuate it as adults. Who doesn't know that aged meat tastes better? Or that a gourmet meal takes a long time to prepare? Anyone knows that spaghetti sauce that has been stewed all day has a much finer quality than something simply dumped out of an instant mix package.

We Will Sell No Wine Before Its Time

Advertisers have known for years that making the customer wait for something enhances the quality of the product. Part of it is the expectation. The savoring of the thought, rather than the experiencing of the fact, is inevitably valuable and can extract a higher price and a greater demand. Consider the popular television commercial of a widely advertised wine that assures the consumer "We will sell no wine before its time." The message is that anything requiring little or no preparation cannot be worth much. We're more than willing to pay a premium price for aged items such as whiskey and wine, meat and cheese. And, to be honest, it does take time to make some things right. But why do we assume *all* things that are good must take time?

Much of what is necessary to "make things right" does take time for physiological reasons. Certainly we would not trust the lawyer who could write us a contract 15 pages long in seven minutes. How could anything possibly be legally sound if it were banged out in only seven minutes?

But much of what we get and pay for and consider good *is* banged out quickly. Your lawyer probably whips out your legal contract from a book of forms. To be sure, he or she will tailor it to your needs, but essentially it's been copied out of a book or taken from a preestablished format. Have you ever compared your will to a friend's will who wants the same bequests as you do? Very similar in language, aren't they?

Have you ever gone into a gourmet restaurant and ordered a meal? The menu advises that "The preparation of fine food takes time." After all, how can you throw some fine food out in front of a customer in three minutes? Obviously, nothing hocus pocus was done to enhance the quality of the gourmet food from ordinary fare. So it takes some *time* to serve you a gourmet meal. Have a drink while you're waiting. Admittedly, that might run up the bar bill, but a good cocktail makes your meal even more succulent—and certainly helps enhance the gross receipts of the restaurant. It's amazing to discover, however, after waiting an hour for your meal to arrive, how quickly it can be replaced if the waiter drops the entree on the floor, or if the food is sent back because it is overcooked, undercooked, or whatever.

How Does This Apply to Managing Others?

While some things *do* require time to develop, mellow, age, or improve, there is certainly no evidence that workers who work slowly, methodically, and procedurally are necessarily doing a better job. To the contrary, most people who work rapidly work better.

Consider the worker who is paid by the job rather than the hour. The hair stylist who cuts four heads of hair in an hour does just as good a job as one who takes the same amount of time to do a single customer; the professional window cleaner who has your windows sparkling in a half-hour may do the same job as someone you hired by the hour and who took a whole day. And almost invariably the typist who can type 100 words per minute has fewer errors than the one who methodically plods along at 50 words per minute. Repetition builds skill and efficiency which, in turn, results in quality.

The problem is that workers use the time theory as leverage in a very self-serving way. Why? Because practically always, when someone gets something finished early, their reward is *more work!* Very seldom does the boss say, "Gee, that's fine. Why don't you take the rest of the day off?" Some bosses do that, but not most. And even with those rare bosses who do, it doesn't happen very often. Because then the boss gets the idea that he or she really doesn't need to pay the employee for the time gone from work and that there isn't enough work to keep the employee busy. So even if you have a boss who's willing to let you go home a little early if you get finished, you don't want to take advantage of that. In other words, if you want something done right, it had *better* take a little time.

Idle Hands Are the Workshop of the Devil

Chapter 4 pointed out the intense need many of us have to do something worthwhile in order to avoid sinning. Bosses and subordinates alike believe that idle hands are the workshop of the devil. Bosses can't stand to see idle subordinates because it creates unproductive payroll time, so they always find something for an idle subordinate to do. Something, no matter what—like redoing what was just done if there isn't anything new to do.

Site: Fort Sill, Oklahoma.   Subject: "Building Character"

To illustrate, return with me to an experience I had in the military at Fort Sill, Oklahoma. After having been out on the rifle range and being familiarized with the latest military weapon of the time, the battery returned to barracks. That was at approximately 1330 hours. The sergeant in charge informed his troops that all they had to do was to clean their weapons and turn them in, at which time they would be free for the day.

Naively believing this cock-and-bull story, I forthrightly disassembled my weapon, cleaned it, reassembled it, and took it to the sergeant for the inspection and turn-in of the rifle. The time now was about 1400 hours.

The sergeant refused to take the rifle when it was offered to him. He immediately assumed a parade rest stance, looked me straight in the eye, and said, "That is the dirtiest, filthiest weapon I've seen in my entire military career. You take it back and you *clean* it before you try to turn it in."

Crestfallen, I returned to the barracks. Knowing I'd already done a pretty thorough job, I thought, "That rifle's clean. The sergeant didn't even really look at it. How could he tell it was the dirtiest rifle in the Army?"

About that time, however, another thought occurred to me—the same thought that has occurred to many soldiers in the service: "The old sergeant goes home every day at 1630 hours. But he can't go home until all those rifles are turned in. By rights, I should be drinking beer right now."

After considering the logic for every bit of two seconds, I decided that it was time to get a beer. I asked if anyone else wanted to go, and another soldier replied, "Yea, I'll go with you." The two of us headed for the PX. Left behind were two filthy rifles.

Interestingly, the PX was located across from the supply shed, and from our vantage point we watched for about an hour and a half. During this time there was quite a parade of soldiers attempting to turn in rifles—all of which apparently were filthy, because out of every three soldiers that would walk in with rifles, there would be three walking back out with rifles. It was a disgrace to the U.S. Army.

However, after about 1600 hours, it became obvious that some of the rifles were finally beginning to get cleaned up. Now there were three men/three rifles going in, three men/two rifles coming out. At about 1615, the ratio changed to three men/three rifles going in, three men/one rifle coming out.

The time was now about 1625. I suggested to the soldier that perhaps our rifles were now clean. The soldier, giving me a particularly astonished look, replied, "Nope, to do a job right takes time. We better have one more beer."

This sounded reasonable to me and, after consuming a fair amount of beer during our research efforts, time didn't seem too important. However, at about 1640 hours, my companion suggested in a definite tone, "*Now* they're clean!"

We both dashed back to our bunks, retrieved our rifles, went to the sergeant, and handed them in. The sergeant, who had been checking the clock, grabbed my rifle, looked down the barrel, and said, "That's more like it, Steinmetz. I hope you learned something from this." The other soldier's rifle was also accepted. And we both learned something from the experience—we had learned how to avoid make-work assignments.

Parkinson's Law and Supervisory Success

Long ago, C. Northcote Parkinson stated the phenomenon that the time required to do a job is roughly equivalent to the time available to do the job.*

People will simply drag out what they are told to do to fill the time available because, inevitably, their reward is simply more work if they get it done ahead of schedule. Therefore, the basic truth that "If something is to be done right, it takes time" has to be reworded.

If something is to be done right, it had *better* take time or otherwise someone's going to think that it was worthless, inept, or otherwise unworthy of being acceptable. Unfortunately, this has a serious debilitating effect on management because bosses are conned into thinking that the slower it goes, the better it is.

Snake oil and hokum notwithstanding, it takes so long to do something. Some things take longer than others, and there are even some things that can't be hurried. But it probably doesn't take as long to do it right as will be allocated its performance—if you're a subordinate who doesn't want to have to do more work for the same amount of pay. And a good boss had better be aware of that fact.

---

* C. Northcote Parkinson, *Parkinson's Law and Other Studies in Administration* (Boston: Houghton Mifflin, 1957).

11

If You Want to Get Ahead, You Need a College Degree

If there is anything spawned from our heritage, it is respect for education. If you want to get ahead, you'd better go to college.

Everyone knows of parents who struggle and save to send their kids to college because they want them to have a better life than they had. And not only does an education result in better jobs, it also gets us "in" with the right people and the right circles. In short, it sets the stage for a lifetime.

Yet it was no less than Mark Twain, a man of letters himself, who is oft quoted as saying, "I tried never to let my schoolin' interfere with my education."

Twain differentiated between the things we learn in the school of hard knocks and the things we learn in the classroom. Just how much did Tom Sawyer learn sitting in school? And did he learn any more or any less skipping school, floating down the Mississippi, exploring the caves outside of Hannibal?

No one would argue that the wonders of electronics, nuclear physics, aeronautical engineering, or medicine are more easily taught in a formalized setting. Still, it is *not* necessarily true that getting ahead requires a college degree.

What's Wrong with the Idea
That if You Want to Get Ahead, You Should Go to College?

These days there are simply too many reasons *not* to believe that people must go to college to get ahead. Point number one is the ambiguity of "getting ahead." Second, no evidence really exists to substantiate a college degree as a prerequisite to success in life. Third, consider an idea summarized in the statement, "It ain't illegal to be stupid."

What Is Getting Ahead?

"Getting ahead" is usually defined as being successful in life along with the usual acquisitions of money, power, fame, glory, and status. But what correlation is there between receipt of a college degree and being the recipient of money, power, fame, glory, or status? Education is not listed in Chapter 6 as a criterion of ascendant-oriented types. Indeed, high educational interest is an attribute found among the ambivalents who, for the most part, are *not* successful by normal measurements.

MBAs vs. Pipefitters: Too Close to Call

Consider the attitudes of high-school graduates who contemplate finding a job or going to college. There are usually two types of high-school seniors: those who expect to go to college and those who don't expect to go to college.

Those who *don't* go to college are often considered failures or drop-outs; while those who expect to pursue a higher education are considered to be "true thinkers" and "right for the world" and "deserving of a successful career." Consider the advantages and disadvantages of education as perceived by the graduating senior. Those who *do* want to go to college (and then on to graduate school, of course) tend to see all kinds of positive consequences of enrolling in and successfully completing a college tour. First off, of course, they will have status, because they "have a college degree." Secondly, they doubtless will make more money—because everybody says they will. Thirdly, they will have the good life of the college campus: intramural activities, scholastic pursuits, and an interesting social life.

Also, many disadvantages are avoided, including such undesirable things as having to go to work (perhaps having to work at an unskilled, low-paying job), having to be financially independent, paying taxes, and missing out on all the fun parties, etc.

And so the picture painted by the parent trying to encourage the youngster to go to college is often irresistible: "Just think what you'll be missing if you don't go to college. It will be so much fun. You'll enjoy every minute of it. You owe it to yourself. Why, I'd have given anything to have had the opportunity to go to college when I was your age . . . ."

On the other hand, if you have ever talked with a high-school senior who does *not* want to go to college, you may have picked up a little different slant about all those "advantages." For example, if you go to college, you will probably be expected to read books, take examinations, and listen to professors discuss stuff that frankly may not have much to do with the real world. Moreover, college may mean you have to associate with people you have little in common with and who you may find dull and boring. You may resent being treated as a child by Mom and Dad who still control the purse strings. You will certainly have to spend a lot of time indoors sitting in classrooms, lecture halls, and laboratories.

Anyone who likes to work with his or her hands, who is outdoor oriented, or who wants to be a manualist by trade is very apt to reject the qualitative aspects of the "good life" to be found at the university. At the same time, he or she is apt to embrace a different set of standards that provide "success." Consider an electrician. If you become an apprentice electrician, you are apt to join the union. Being in the union, you are going to meet a lot of nice people who really understand what the world is all about. Furthermore, electricians get to work with their hands, and they get to work on "real jobs" such as construction where they can see what they're accomplishing. In addition, electricians can make a *lot* of money, even apprentice electricians.

Also consider the starting wages of an apprentice electrician and a school teacher. At the time of this writing, an apprentice electrician makes $21,735 per year working a 50-week year straight time in Boulder, Colorado. That electrician can be age 18 and fresh out of high school. A teacher fresh out of college in

Boulder, Colorado will make $11,418. But, of course, that is for a school year—so they may make an additional $1,920 in the summer (average) to bring their total to $13,338 for the year.

But comparing teachers (whom everyone *knows* are underpaid) to "real people" is ridiculous. So let's look at the "creme de la creme" of the 1980s: the petroleum engineer. The petroleum engineer fresh out of school can expect to make $26,244 per year according to the College Placement Council Salary Survey at the time of this writing—a whopping $4,509 per year more than our electrician who is five years younger. (The apprentice electrician is 18; the new petroleum engineer is 23.) Our 23-year-old electrician will make $28,980 per year, or $2,736 per year *more* than the petroleum engineer at the same age (23)—*and will have accumulated earnings for five years* of approximately $130,000, while the petroleum engineer will have cost whoever supported him or her in college about $30,000 for an education at a *state-supported* institution.

Thus, by age 23, the petroleum engineer stands score 0; the apprentice electrician stands score $160,000 (not to mention *not* having been tax supported) *and* is making $2,736 per year *more* than our petroleum engineer.

But our petroleum engineer *will* catch up. We know that is true because everyone says so—and the statistics bear it out. By age 51, our electrician and our petroleum engineer will be virtually even (assuming, of course, that the petroleum engineer is as valuable to society then as at the time of this writing—not necessarily a valid assumption). Incidentally, at age 51, our school teacher can expect to make $26,000 per year.

One fundamental problem, then, with getting ahead by going to college is that "getting ahead" may not occur for the person who likes to work with his or her hands, who likes to be physically involved in doing things, who enjoys experiences of being a doer rather than a manager, and who sees no shame in being a "working stiff."

The Evidence Just Isn't There

A second reason to question the necessity of a college education in relation to "getting ahead" is that there is no particular evidence the two are related in terms of money, power, fame, or glory. Indeed, education simply does not necessarily ensure any of those attributes, which tend to fall on those who are manualists endowed with certain physical and manipulative skills that they capitalize on. Sound like a lot of double talk? Well, consider the following statistics.

According to *Business Week*, 25 executives in 1980 earned more than $1 million per year running corporations. In virtually all cases they were the president, or chairman of the board, or a combination of the two—*and* had college degrees. They probably also have money, status, and possibly even some fame and glory. But that's only 25 out of a population of executives and managers in the United States that would push at least 100,000 and out of a working force of 15.5 million college graduates.*

In contrast to the executives who have really hit it big, consider how many professional entertainers have achieved the same power, money, fame, glory, and status. How many entertainers are there who make a million dollars a year or more? You could probably name 25 simply by reading this week's television schedule or by casually glancing through the movie listings in the entertainment section of your local newspaper.

When you have exhausted television personalities and movie stars, think of professional athletes. More than 25 of them make $1 million annually, and many of them crowd that seven-digit figure awfully close. Indeed, in 1980 the average salary of (low paid, relatively speaking) baseball players was $150,000 per year.**

Even in the Professional World, the Evidence Isn't There

What about the so-called professional class? What parents aren't proud of their offspring who become doctors? There's no denying the fact that medical doctors have status in our society, but they don't often achieve fame and glory, and their hours are often long and tedious because accidents and sickness don't seem to occur eight to five, Monday through Friday. Yet despite all their many years of education, dedication, and long hours of hard work, there are still very few medical doctors with earned

---

* U.S. Dept. of Commerce, Bureau of Census.
** "Baseball Bosses Toss a Curve," *Business Week*, May 4, 1981, p. 168.

incomes of more than $1 million per year. The plight of lawyers, architects, engineers, dentists, and accountants is worse.

It Ain't Illegal to Be Stupid

The third reason not to buy into the "truth" of the value of a college degree is best summarized in the statement "It ain't illegal to be stupid."

If you're stupid, you'll be protected. If you number among the ignorant, poor, or downtrodden who are being taken advantage of by our society, rest assured that you nevertheless will live in moderate comfort. If you're smart, you're hurtin' because nobody is going to help you.

While it is true that our judicial system is not as sympathetic to hardened criminals who commit violent crimes (although that can be argued, too), it is also true that our justice system is rather lenient on those who "don't understand" that they were supposed to file income taxes or that they were supposed to have financial liability insurance coverage. If you don't believe that, try to cop the same plea about filing your taxes while wearing your Phi Beta Kappa key from State University. You try it and you will be hurting, because everybody knows you are smart and successful. And while you may not have money and power, you certainly have an option on fame, glory, or status. So pay up, Buddy. You are successful. You went to college.

You *are* successful, aren't you?

12

Good Workers Make Good Supervisors

This "truth" is probably the least discussed but one of the most common. It embodies the old idea that your really dedicated, loyal, hard-working, conscientious, competent, high performer is the one who knows what needs to be done and can effectively instill these traits in those he or she supervises.

The problem is that we invariably want to reward our high-level performers and, above and beyond monetary rewards, there isn't much we can do that does not involve a supervisory appointment. We can give them better working conditions, more vacation or leave time, various benefits and privileges, the softer job, the work station by the window or furthest from the washroom or closest to the water cooler. But all of these tokens of appreciation, if not associated with some titular change, inevitably become viewed as favoritism.

What's Wrong with Favoritism?

Many experienced supervisors and managers feel there isn't a thing wrong with giving special benefits to those employees who produce the most. If you've got a crackerjack performer, allow him or her to knock off early. If someone really does a wonderful job, praise him or her in a staff meeting. If an individual is especially thorough or competent, give him or her a public commendation. This is simply good motivational practice, isn't it? Well, the answer is no, it isn't. Giving recognition or certain benefits or privileges is *not* a poor motivational tactic, but inevitably the recipient—particularly if it's almost always the same person—is perceived as being a favorite of the boss and various antagonisms develop.

But antagonism isn't the whole problem. Inevitably, it seems that the other employees, who aren't getting the recognition, favors, etc., are motivated to do something debilitating to the recipient. And therefore, some employees who receive that recognition become somewhat disdainful of it. Moreover, they sometimes feel that they are being "leaned on" by the boss to perform better but really have no defenses or protection from fellow workers.

So It All Comes Down to a Promotion

So what happens, ultimately, is that the manager gives a little authority, along with recognition, to the best worker. This doesn't necessarily mean a promotion to a "supervisor"—it often simply means designating that employee as a lead person or senior operator, which then gives him or her some clout. That highly performing individual is put in a position of not having to be part of the rank-and-file; somehow they are "better." But this invariably carries some supervisory responsibility. So, whether we like it or not, we end up making supervisors out of our better workers.

Good Workers Don't Necessarily Make Good Supervisors

The problem with making good workers into supervisors is that there is no assurance that even the best workers will be adequate as supervisors. Being a good doer doesn't necessarily ensure that one will be a good manager. Often those who are good at "doing" work don't know *why* they are good at it and cannot necessarily impart expertise on doing that job to those they supervise or train. Also, some good workers don't relate that well with other workers and/or don't necessarily like to share the specialized knowledge or techniques that make them good doers. This often occurs in highly specialized, technical jobs. Therefore, we end up making our very best workers into our absolute *worst* supervisors.

What Makes Good Supervisors?

Any basic primer on supervisory practices will indicate that good supervision requires, among others, skills in the following areas:

- Human relations skills, including working not only with individuals but small groups of people.
- Communications skills, including written, oral, formal, and informal (grapevine).
- Leadership skills, including the ability to motivate employees and harness talents of subordinates.
- Skills at coping with "Big Brother," i.e., the union and all the labor relations matters.
- Performance appraisal and evaluation skills, including coaching, counseling, and disciplinary talent.
- Skills at training employees to do technical work.
- Order-giving capability—especially with an ability to not antagonize those receiving the orders.
- Ability to cope with griping and grievances.
- A special knack to handle minority relationship-type problems, such as relating with sexist problems, younger or older employee disputes, racial antagonisms, handicapped persons, etc.
- Facility at handling troublemakers and the extraordinarily difficult employee who seems to delight in wreaking havoc within the organization.
- Knowledge of planning and scheduling, including such things as reading blueprints, drawings, or otherwise detailed instructions.
- Knowledge of how to control costs, including how costs are incurred and how they can be minimized.
- Concern over housekeeping and maintenance.
- Coping with such employee behavior as passing the buck, complacency, etc.
- Coping with intracompany politics.

Note that there just *isn't very much* listed that relates to "doing jobs," such as facility and speed at operating a machine, materials handling, using jig and fixtures, spraying and coating, answering the telephone, typing a letter, waiting on a customer, programming a computer, etc. Page 96 shows a sample list of the "doing" activities from one page in the *Dictionary of Occupational Titles*, which lists approximately 20,000 "doing" activities.

The matter is rather simple. People who excel at "doing" work are not necessarily equipped to be good supervisors. This is why first-line supervisory training programs are so in demand throughout the United States. People are rewarded for being good doers by getting appointed to jobs they are ill-equipped to handle. They are often thrown into that job under the assumption that they can develop the supervisory skills necessary to do an adequate job and/or under the erroneous belief that their technical skills will supersede all supervisory skills and enable them to become successful.

The facts are that if good employees are to make good supervisors, they have to be *trained* successfully at using supervisory skills. They cannot simply rely on the talent and skill that produced their success in the past. Employees do not make good supervisors unless adequate training is provided.

Some People Don't Know Why They Are Good

Even if supervisory success were attainable as a direct result of technical competency on the job, some people still don't *know* why they are as competent as they are.

We've all watched a crane operator positioning a beam or a pipe, or seen a backhoe operator digging a trench, or marveled at an extremely accurate typist pounding out 120 words per minute, letter perfect, *ad infinitum*. These people often don't know why they can do their job so well. Usually they just assume it's a God-given trait, the result of some "gift" they have, or accept the fact that it is a knack or physical or psychomotor dexterity that enables them to be so proficient. Often they say that "Anyone can do it who's been at it as long as I have." But the fact is they can't really explain it.

But they cannot impart this skill to others. It is not at all unusual to see this phenomenon in the arts and entertainment field. How many Picassos, Rembrandts, and Michelangelos have taught young artists to be Picassos, Rembrandts, and Michelangelos? How many of the talented singers, actors, dancers, comediennes, etc. have successfully taught others to sing, dance, act, or tell jokes? Many of them will simply say, "You stand up and do it," or they might say that they learned what they know from a voice coach, music teacher, drama class, etc. But they can't tell you why it is and how it is that *they* can do it well. And there are any number of successful actors, entertainers, and the like who haven't *ever* been particularly schooled or trained. They just started doing it, learned to do it well, are good at it, or just accidentally stumbled into being good at it, and that's that.

Appointing someone as a supervisor because they can do something well is not necessarily going to ensure that the people they supervise will also learn to do that task well. Practically always the best they can do is say "Copy me," "Do it the way I do it," "Watch me again and I think maybe you'll get the knack of it." Such leadership, in the eyes of the subordinate, is not helpful. Furthermore, if the supervisor is especially good at doing the job, it is intimidating and inhibiting to the subordinate, who feels helpless and hopelessly unable to master the doing task that is being taught.

Some People Won't Share Their Knowledge

Another group *does* know why they are good, but *will not* share that information with the subordinates that they are supposed to train.

There are practically always little tricks to use and perfect that make a job infinitely easier to do. For example, consider the job of the proofreader. Most people proofread to correct errors by reading the manuscript in the usual way: that is, from left to right. But a good proofreader knows that, to spot errors, one should read the copy backwards. They are far more apt to spot errors that way—but why tell a new employee that? Let him or her figure it out alone.

ALPHABETICAL INDEX OF OCCUPATIONAL TITLES

CELL STRIPPER (plastics mat.) 556.686-014
cell stripper, final (plastics mat.) 556.587-010
CELL TENDER (chem.) 558.382-026
CELL-TENDER HELPER (chem.) 558.685-022
CELL TESTER (chem.) 558.584-010
CELL TUBER, HAND (elec. equip.) 727.687-046
CELL TUBER, MACHINE (elec. equip.) 692.685-046
CELLULOID TRIMMER (sports equip.) 732.684-046
CEMENT-BOAT-AND-BARGE LOADER (cement) 921.665-010
CEMENT-CAR DUMPER (const.) 579.665-014
CEMENT-CONVEYOR OPERATOR (const.) 579.665-014
cementer (any ind.) 795.687-014
cementer (any ind.) 780.684-062
cementer (auto. ser.) 750.684-038
cementer (leather mfg.) 585.687-022
CEMENTER (optical goods) 711.684-014
CEMENTER (pen & pencil) 733.687-030
CEMENTER (ship & boat bldg. & rep.) 844.364-010
CEMENTER AND FOLDER, MACHINE (boot & shoe) 690.685-070
CEMENTER FOR FOLDING, MACHINE (boot & shoe) 690.686-018
CEMENTER, HAND (boot & shoe) 788.687-030
CEMENTER HELPER (petrol. production) 939.684-018
CEMENTER, MACHINE (boot & shoe) 692.685-050
cementer, machine (leather prod.) 690.686-022
CEMENTER, MACHINE APPLICATOR (boot & shoe) 690.686-018
CEMENTER, MACHINE JOINER (boot & shoe) 690.685-074
CEMENTER, OIL WELL (petrol. production) 939.462-010
cement finisher (const.) 844.364-010
cement-finisher apprentice (const.) 844.364-014
CEMENT-FINISHING SUPERVISOR (const.) 869.131-014
CEMENT FITTINGS MAKER (conc. prod.) 779.684-010
CEMENT-GUN OPERATOR (conc. prod.; const.) 849.665-010
CEMENT HANDLER (const.) 579.665-014
CEMENT LOADER (cement) 921.565-010
CEMENT MASON (const.) 844.364-010
CEMENT-MASON APPRENTICE (const.) 844.364-014
CEMENT-MASON HELPER (const.) 869.687-026
CEMENT MASON, HIGHWAYS AND STREETS (const.) 869.664-014
CEMENT MASON, MAINTENANCE (any ind.) 844.364-010
cement mixer (cement) 570.685-010
CEMENT MIXER (rubber goods; rubber tire & tube) 550.685-026
cement patcher (conc. prod.) 844.684-010
cement paver (const.) 844.364-010
CEMENT-RAILROAD-CAR LOADER (cement) 921.565-010
cement rubber (conc. prod.) 844.684-010
CEMENT-SACK BREAKER (const.) 579.665-014
CEMENT SPRAYER HELPER, NOZZLE (conc. prod.; const.)
CEMENT SPRAYER, NOZZLE (conc. prod.; const.) 869.664-014
cement-storage worker (cement) 579.685-050
CEMENT TESTER (cement) 029.261-010
CEMENT-TILE MAKER (conc. prod.) 579.685-042
CEMENT-TRUCK LOADER (cement) 921.565-010
CEMETERY WORKER (real estate) 406.684-010
CENSUS CLERK (gov. ser.) 216.382-062
CENSUS ENUMERATOR (gov. ser.) 205.367-054
CENTERLESS-GRINDER OPERATOR, PRODUCTION (mach. shop)
603.685-062
CENTERLESS-GRINDING-MACHINE ADJUSTER (ammunition)
626.281-010
centerless-grinding-machine operator (mach. shop) 603.382-014
CENTER-LINE-CUTTER OPERATOR (const.) 853.663-014
CENTER-MACHINE OPERATOR (confection.) 520.682-014
center maker, hand (confection.) 520.684-014
CENTER-PUNCH OPERATOR (phonograph) 690.685-078
CENTER-SECTION ASSEMBLER (aircraft-aerospace mfg.) 769.281-
010
CENTRAL-AIR-CONDITIONING INSTALLER (any ind.) 827.464-010
CENTRAL-CONTROL-ROOM OPERATOR (light, heat, & power)
952.362-042
CENTRAL-OFFICE EQUIPMENT ENGINEER (tel. & tel.) 003.187-
010
CENTRAL-OFFICE INSTALLER (tel. & tel.) 822.361-014
central-office maintainer (tel. & tel.) 822.281-014
CENTRAL-OFFICE OPERATOR (tel. & tel.) 235.462-010
CENTRAL-OFFICE-OPERATOR SUPERVISOR (tel. & tel.) 235.132-
010
CENTRAL-OFFICE REPAIRER (tel. & tel.) 822.281-014
CENTRAL-OFFICE-REPAIRER SUPERVISOR (tel. & tel.) 822.131-
010
CENTRAL-OFFICE SUPERVISOR (tel. & tel.) 822.131-010
central-supply aide (medical ser.) 381.687-010
CENTRAL-SUPPLY WORKER (medical ser.) 381.687-010

CENTRIFUGAL-CASTING-MACHINE OPERATOR (jewelry)
502.682-018
CENTRIFUGAL-CASTING-MACHINE OPERATOR (found.) I
514.685-010
CENTRIFUGAL-CASTING-MACHINE OPERATOR (found.) II
514.685-014
CENTRIFUGAL-CASTING-MACHINE OPERATOR (found.) III
514.562-010
CENTRIFUGAL-CASTING-MACHINE TENDER (button) 556.385-
010
CENTRIFUGAL-DRIER OPERATOR (chem.) 551.685-026
centrifugal-extractor operator (any ind.) 581.685-038
CENTRIFUGAL OPERATOR (corn prod.; sugar) 521.682-010
CENTRIFUGAL-SCREEN TENDER (paper & pulp) 533.685-022
CENTRIFUGAL SEPARATOR (choc. & cocoa) 521.685-070
CENTRIFUGAL SPINNER (conc. prod.) 575.664-010
CENTRIFUGAL-STATION OPERATOR, AUTOMATIC (sugar)
521.585-010
centrifugal supervisor (sugar) 529.130-042
CENTRIFUGAL-WAX MOLDER (found.; jewelry) 549.685-038
centrifuge operator (chem.) 551.685-026
CENTRIFUGE OPERATOR (chew. gum) 521.685-026
CENTRIFUGE OPERATOR (corn prod.) 521.685-046
CENTRIFUGE OPERATOR (dairy prod.) 521.685-042
CENTRIFUGE OPERATOR (distilled liquors; malt liquors) 521.685-
118
CENTRIFUGE OPERATOR (oils & fats) 521.685-050
CENTRIFUGE OPERATOR (paint & varn.) 551.685-034
CENTRIFUGE OPERATOR (soap) 551.685-030
CENTRIFUGE OPERATOR, PLASMA PROCESSING (drug. prep. &
rel. prod.; medical ser.) 599.685-018
CENTRIFUGE-SEPARATOR OPERATOR (glue) 551.685-038
CENTRIFUGE-SEPARATOR TENDER (nonfer. metal alloys) 541.585-
010
CEPHALOMETRIC ANALYST (medical ser.) 078.384-010
cephalometric technician (medical ser.) 078.384-010
cephalometric tracer (medical ser.) 078.384-010
CERAMIC CAPACITOR PROCESSOR (electronics) 590.684-010
CERAMIC COATER, MACHINE (any ind.) 509.685-022
CERAMIC DESIGN ENGINEER (profess. & kin.) 006.061-010
CERAMIC ENGINEER (profess. & kin.) 006.061-014
CERAMIC-MAKER DEMONSTRATOR (ret. tr.) 297.354-010
ceramic plater (any ind.) 509.685-022
CERAMIC RESEARCH ENGINEER (profess. & kin.) 006.061-018
CERAMIC SPRAYER (brick & tile, pottery & porc.) 741.684-026
ceramics technician (medical ser.) 712.281-010
CERAMICS TEST ENGINEER (profess. & kin.) 006.061-022
ceramist (medical ser.) 712.281-010
cereal miller (cereal) 521.682-022
cereal popper (cereal) 523.382-010
CERROBEND-DIE CASTER (aircraft-aerospace mfg.) 502.381-014
CERTIFICATION AND SELECTION SPECIALIST (education)
099.167-010
certified public accountant (profess. & kin.) see ACCOUNTANT,
CERTIFIED PUBLIC
certified welder (welding) see WELDER, CERTIFIED
CHAIN BUILDER, LOOM CONTROL (textile) 683.381-010
chainer (textile) 683.381-010
CHAIN-FORMING-MACHINE OPERATOR (forging) 612.462-010
CHAIN-HOIST OPERATOR (mining & quarrying) 921.663-026
chain-machine operator (needle, pin, & rel. prod.) 692.685-270
CHAIN MAKER, HAND (jewelry) 700.381-010
chain maker, loom control (textile) 683.381-010
CHAIN MAKER, MACHINE (jewelry) 700.684-022
CHAIN MENDER (jewelry) 735.687-014
CHAIN-MORTISER OPERATOR (woodworking) 665.482-014
CHAIN OFFBEARER (plan. mill; sawmill) 669.686-018
chain pegger (textile) 683.381-010
CHAIN REPAIRER (carpet & rug) 683.684-010
chain-saw mechanic (any ind.) 625.281-030
CHAINSAW OPERATOR (logging, veneer & plywood; wood distil. &
char.) 454.687-010
chain splitter (textile) 683.381-010
CHAINSTITCH SEWING MACHINE OPERATOR (garment) 786.682-
054
CHAIN-TESTING-MACHINE OPERATOR (forging) 616.685-010
CHAIR INSPECTOR (furn.) 763.687-026
CHAIR INSPECTOR AND LEVELER (furn.) 763.687-014
CHAIRPERSON, SCHOLARSHIP AND LOAN COMMITTEE
(education) 090.117-030
chair-post-machine operator (furn.) 669.682-022
CHAIR-SPRING ASSEMBLER (furn.) 780.684-098
chair trimmer (furn.) 780.684-034
CHAIR UPHOLSTERER (furn.) 780.684-034

991

Motivation Is Not Equal to Leadership

The basic fault with the "truth" that good workers make good supervisors is that those who appoint good workers to be good supervisors often assume that physical facility and skill at doing a job can be easily imparted from one person to the other. It is complicated by the tendency to believe that motivation is essentially what is necessary to get someone to do a good job.

But *motivation is not equal to leadership.* Leadership skills come about by being competent at performing supervisor's tasks—*not* from being a good doer. It never has, and it never will.

However, because it is difficult to reward good "doers" without eventually promoting them to supervisory positions, we must deal with this problem as a fact of life. It is therefore recommended that "doers" who are to assume a supervisory position be given adequate and complete supervisory training *before* they assume their new responsibilities.

13

A Good Boss Will Always Take An Active Interest in What Employees Do— Both On and Off the Job

Another fantasy about "good" bosses is that they must care for, understand, be concerned with, and generally treat their employees as mature adults.

Unfortunately, except for on-the-job activities, this belief is as unsupportable in practice as it could be. Indeed, if it is believed, the boss probably lacks any valid managerial experience and tries instead to communicate to the rest of the world how he feel things *ought* to be in an ideal setting.

Certainly we need superiors to tell us *good things*, to give us hope, to lead us to believe there is a better way. Unfortunately, this strategy has a limited practical application in business.

Why Shouldn't a Good Boss Take An Active Interest in Employees?

A good boss should *not* take an active interest in what employees do because the very thing that this interest is supposed to instill will be frustrated by the activity itself. A "good boss's" interest in employees is to demonstrate the sincere, genuine concern held for the individual. Asking about activities, plans, or personal interests presumably makes the boss somewhat more human, and also elevates the employee to a higher personal level in the boss–employee relationship …or so the theory goes.

Advocates of the "personal interest" theory make the analogy to good parenting. Parents who have good relationships with their children are not much different from bosses who have good relationships with employees. The sincere, genuinely interested parent knows what the child is doing, understands and respects the child, and reciprocally receives respect back from the child. Likewise, the boss receives the same respect in the superior–subordinate relationship. However, do we want an employee to be a child?

Meddling

Now, there is simply no question but that managing others by taking an active interest in their non-work-type activities is going to create problems. Those problems will come from employees who perceive the boss as meddling.

The facts are that most people resent the intrusion of inquisitive acquaintances at work, whether the inquirer is a boss, a co-worker, or a subordinate. Somehow, however, the intrusion is most resented when it is the boss asking, because one never knows the ulterior motives of the high and mighty.

As pointed out in Chapter 9, it may be that the boss simply wants to trick the employee into working harder. Or it may be that the boss is interested in certain lecherous possibilities and is deviously inquiring about the prospects. Or perhaps the boss is naive and insensitive to the employee's privacy. Or is the boss trying to blackmail, prod, goad, or otherwise psychologically manipulate some kind of behavior from the subordinate? These and other possibilities run through the employees' minds.

So there's no question that "asking after" employees becomes meddlesome. But the problem doesn't end with the meddling.

Familiarity Breeds Contempt

Bosses who decide it is their duty to know everything about their subordinates are probably going to induce a great deal of hostility and antagonism. Why else would we have laws that sanctify the privacy of the individual? The answer must be that some people don't want some things made public knowledge, because such knowledge may lead to devastating results in their superior–subordinate relationship and employment conditions.

By way of example, consider a situation that occurred several years ago in an organization where several newly hired individuals were required to work for, and report to, the same direct supervisor. One individual slowly became an outcast to the organization because he was an independent cuss, to some degree a loner, and the kind of individual who "liked to stand on his own two feet." In addition, he felt it was not particularly desirable as an employee to be too dependent upon the supervisor, opting rather to fight his own battles and win his own way in the world.

After approximately one year it became painfully obvious to this individual that he was not making the kind of progress that his peers were making. This was underscored by a salary review that resulted in a minimal raise, coupled by a poor performance evaluation. As he lamented his plight to the others in the organization who had been hired at the same time, one fellow worker suggested that the problem was that the person did not take any of his problems to the supervisor.

The individual seemed astonished by this observation and asked why that might create a problem. His co-worker said it should be obvious that all the other people in the group concocted, contrived, manufactured, and otherwise fabricated personal problems and difficulties, questions about their career advancement, and other extraneous personal activity/involvement circumstances. These they would take to the supervisor and lay them on the table so the supervisor could (a) know what's going on, (b) get some inside knowledge about the personal problems of the subordinates, and (c) advise the subordinates on what to do.

The only problem with the supervisor was that every now and again she would expect the subordinate to take her advice. However, there was practically always some logical reason why the advice could not or should not be taken. Or, a miraculous recovery, cure, reconciliation, appeasement, or other "It's all better" circumstance could arise so that the subordinate would not be overly obligated to institute the advice given by the supervisor.

After this advice was given to the poorly performing individual, there was a marked change in his relationship with his supervisor. He began to develop problems and difficulties. And he saw reason to ask the experience-wise supervisor for her advice and counsel. Virtually overnight, the subordinate began to be elevated in stature to an equal among peers in his group. Within a period of about six months, he had indeed surpassed the standing of the majority of his peers. But then he quit his job. Said he couldn't stand all the butting in, unneeded advice, unwarranted inferences, and public airing of personal (albeit not necessarily real) problems.

The Troops Need Privacy
from the Sergeant in the Barracks

Maybe an old military principle begins to carry the day with respect to the fundamental truth that a good boss will always take an active interest in his or her employees, in what they're doing both on and off the job. In the service it is considered that under the best and worst conditions, people need to have some kind of privacy. It may be true that a squad leader sleeps in the barracks with the troops, but that squad leader will have a private room or be otherwise segregated in some way. The reason is that all the troops want some privacy. And obtaining privacy often is facilitated by the absence of the boss.

If familiarity does not breed contempt, it does tend to enable one to know just where and how to insert the pinpoint to most antagonize one's adversaries, put them down, burst their balloon, or flat-out cripple them. People who have lived together for years can have the very best fights of all. They know just how to say *the* word; just *what* funny look to have on their faces; just what pitiful *tone* of voice to use to drive the other person up the wall. Supervisors and subordinates seldom develop that kind of talent—if they don't get too close to each other. Thus, they don't lose the respect for each other that is necessary in a superior–subordinate relationship. So even if you're tempted to show an interest in your employees' personal lives—resist. If they want you to know what they're doing, they'll tell you.

14

A Highly Motivated Worker
Is More Effective
Than One Who Isn't

Any book on managerial truth must deal with the subject of motivation—and any book on motivation must face up to the question of what motivates workers and why one worker is not as motivated as another.

Everyone seems to agree that a highly motivated worker is a more effective worker, that someone who is motivated is going to try harder. Therefore, individuals who are interested in their work will be more successful. Or so the thinking goes.

Is a Highly Motivated
Worker Really More Effective?

Hold on! Surely a truth as fundamental as this can't be dissected. Before continuing, take the test on page 106. It's quite simple: All you have to do is connect, in normal counting sequence, all the numbers on the page, starting with 1 and ending with 48. But before taking the test, read the following guidelines:

All the numbers from 1 through 48 are on the page.
No numbers have been omitted.

No numbers have been duplicated.

Note the following standards:

    a. A decent average time is 1 minute, 30 seconds.

    b. Failing time is more than 2 minutes.

    c. Record time is about 42 seconds.

    Only two things count: speed and accuracy. It makes no difference what it looks like. So now get a watch and a pencil and take the test; then record the time it takes you to complete the test.

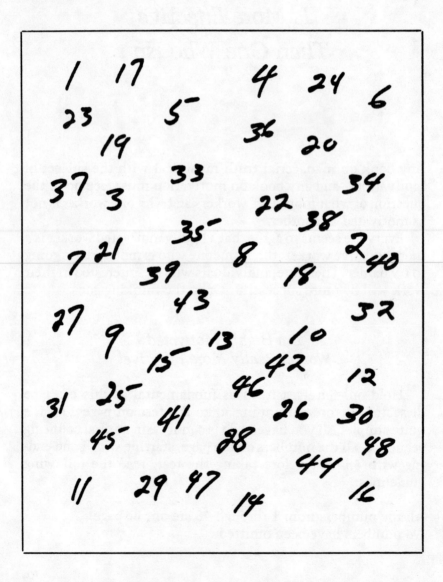

So Why Did You Fail?

You probably failed. Why? Were you not motivated to do the test in at least standard time? Odds are if you're simply a motivated person who's trying to "do your job," you probably took anywhere from 2 to 5 minutes to successfully complete the test. If that is true, what went wrong?

Some People Try Too Hard

One of the reasons why many people fail is that they are *too highly* motivated—they try *too* hard. It's like the person who wants to make sure the equipment holds together and ends up popping the head off a bolt or stripping the threads while tightening a nut. What is it about motivation that causes people to be overly motivated? Does overmotivation lead to less than satisfactory performance? Does too much attention to detail distort the overall picture? Often it does.

Sometimes the Obvious Isn't So Obvious

Sometimes people are so highly motivated that they lose their effectiveness. Sometimes, too, people are so overly anxious that they don't bother to stand back and assess the situation.

Anyone familiar with numbers should be able to look at the test and immediately see that the odd numbers are on the left side of the page and the even numbers are on the right side of the page. This knowledge will virtually assure successful performance in under 2 minutes—and you can walk and chew gum at the same time!

But the instructions didn't *say* that the odds were on the left and the evens were on the right. And even if the instructions had said so, the test taker may not have heeded the instructions. How many times have you seen the old trick test that starts with item #1, which states, "Before doing anything else, read all the items on this page," and then, rather than following those instructions carefully, the test taker proceeds to do all the idiotic itemized things as instructed—such as yelling out loud, clapping hands, dancing around the chair, etc.—before arriving at the last item on the page, which says,

"Ignore all of the above instructions and sit silently in your seat."

Intelligence Helps, Too

An effective worker is intelligent and informed, rather than simply highly motivated. For example, if you really want to successfully complete the numbers test, you not only need to know that the odds are on the left and the evens are on the right; you also need to know that the first eight numbers (1–8) are on the top half of the page, the second eight (9–16) are on the bottom, the third eight (17-24) are on the top, the fourth eight (25-32) are on the bottom, the fifth set of eight numbers (33–40) are on the top, and the last set of eight (41–48) are on the bottom. Thus, if you know that (a) the page can be arranged in quadrants, (b) the odds are on the left and the evens are on the right, and (c) that one goes from top to bottom for each series of eight, you should easily be able to do the test in 1 minute 30 seconds—normal for a first "informed" try.

Nobody Told Me

Again, the reader is going to yell foul. "Nobody told me that the odds are on the left or the evens are on the right, and that isn't as obvious as it might seem. Furthermore, how could I intuitively observe that the first eight are on the top, the next eight are on the bottom, etc.?"

Nobody said anything about the duty of a boss, a spouse, or an author to play fair. Admittedly, the instructions weren't there—but that was to point out that intelligence and information are *far more significant* than motivation when it comes to successfully doing a job.

Doctors Don't Do Surgery
on Members of Their Immediate Family

People who are objective tend to be more relaxed under pressure, to keep their wits about them, and to perform better. To paraphrase Jim Bouton in his book *Ball Four*, when there are two out in the last of the ninth, the score tied, the bases loaded, and the pitcher makes ready to deliver what may very well be the final pitch of the World Series, the only way to tell the difference between a professional and an amateur is that the professional views it as simply one more pitch, while the amateur is so up-tight that he may very well throw the ball 15 feet over the third baseman's head and not even in the direction of the catcher. Nerves have one heck of a lot to do with effectiveness. And high motivation tends to create nerves that are not conducive to effective performance.

Some Lawyers Have Fools for Clients

The "truth" of another fundamental precept arises from the same logic. We cannot be committed emotionally to an issue and maintain the kind of objectivity necessary to perform professionally. Too many things go wrong; too many emotions cause us to lose sight of the true objective. Vision gets clouded because of overreaction or underreaction.

On Dishonest Motivation

Some of us are motivated to do a job to the satisfaction of ourselves or our own standards rather than to the satisfaction of our boss. Remember the story about the little old lady in Iowa who worked in a bank for decades who very slowly and methodically embezzled more than $1 million before she was discovered?

Was the embezzler effective? Indeed, she was successful in lifting over $1 million from the bank. Was she motivated? She was extremely highly motivated. Did she accomplish her job well? She accomplished her job very well—but the stockholders still weren't very pleased with her.

Even When You're Motivated Right, Things Can Go Wrong

"OK," you say, "so occasionally there's a rotten apple. Basically, most people are honest and well-intentioned."

This reminds me of the platoon of men who were not "falling out" to a platoon sergeant's satisfaction. He became greatly distressed and, exerting every leadership capability, strategy, and tactic he could muster, gave a pep talk to the troops, saying that the entire platoon should be able to fall out of the barracks within a period of one minute. The sergeant offered this time as a challenge to the entire platoon, who willingly agreed to see if they could satisfactorily perform in the required time.

So the platoon went into the barracks to wait for the order to fall out, but unfortunately did not quite make it in acceptable time. They then agreed to try again, with the same result. Consequently, it was agreed to try a third time. By this time all the troops were truly interested in satisfying the sergeant (and, needless to say, tired of running in and out). So, after going back into the barracks, they all agreed that, rather than lounge around on their bunks waiting for the inevitable command, they would simply line up behind the door and wait for the order. After all, they knew full well it wouldn't be too long before the sergeant would give the call.

Sure enough, a few minutes later the sergeant gave the command to fall out, at which time the thundering herd came out. Unfortunately, the second man out the door tripped and fell, and the rest of the entire platoon ran over him and broke his arm. They did get out the door in the required amount of time. But were they effective? Well, they accomplished the objective—but succeeded in throwing the baby out with the bathwater at the same time.

So You Want To Be a Skydiver

One last example is in order to really describe motivation as it relates to job effectiveness. First, take another test.

Instructions: Immediately after reading the following question, write your answer to the question in the space provided below.

Question: If you were going to be a skydiver, who would pack your parachute?

If you answered the question "I would," you are probably not only a poor delegator (see Chapters 2 and 5), you are also unwilling to accept the fact that motivation has little, if anything, to do with how effectively a job is done.

For example, if you said that you would pack your own parachute, I would have to ask you what you know about packing parachutes. If your answer is "Nothing, but I'll learn!" you are simply arguing the question that your *motivation* to learn how to do a job right will probably cause you to be more successful than someone trained and experienced in packing parachutes. In other words, you're arguing that your inherent motivation to pack your own parachute will make you more successful than the desire for a professional parachute rigger to do a *professional* job.

Most parachutes that are jumped are, in fact, rigged by a licensed rigger. Indeed, many states have laws requiring that licensed riggers pack chutes (rather than unlicensed, albeit highly motivated, skydivers).

So Another Truth Bites the Dust

There are many examples of the problems of overmotivation that make us somewhat less effective than we might otherwise be. It is very comforting to think that someone who is highly motivated is going to be effective. But there is no more reason to believe that motivation is going to make one effective than there is to believe that since trees grow up from the ground they will, therefore, naturally grow to the sky.

No argument is made here that *lack of motivation* will cause someone to be effective. And no particular denial is made that one who is motivated is apt to try a little harder and therefore perhaps succeed a little better. But one who is extremely highly motivated is often more likely to be an ineffective performer. Furthermore, the numbers test should have demonstrated that even in those situations where modest motivation exists one may nevertheless fail.

So another basic truth bites the dust. Motivation *isn't* necessarily going to make subordinates more effective. Indeed, it may make them miserable flops at their jobs if they are too highly motivated. And even if they are moderately motivated, they may fail through ignorance or lack of information.

The upshot of the entire problem can be summarized in the cliché "The road to hell is paved with good intentions." There simply isn't any evidence to substantiate that motivation *per se* is sufficient to cause anyone to do an acceptable, satisfactory, or effective job. Motivation can cause people to clench up; motivation can cause people to overkill; motivation can lead to absolute disaster.

15

Employees' Attitude
Is What Counts

Tradition has maintained that workers with good attitudes are productive and therefore desirable to have around, while those with bad attitudes are less productive and probably hard to manage.

How to Modify Behavior

Behavior modificationists argue that if you can control what happens to an employee, you can shape that employee's attitude toward a working situation. Once you shape a person's attitude toward a working condition, you can control the worker's behavior. After all, behavior is a function of attitude plus facts of the situation.

Behavior = Attitude + Facts

This formula simply states that if one's attitude is "good," the boss is more likely to get good behavior than if one's attitude is "bad."

Of course, the facts of the situation have to be considered, too. Someone may have a good attitude but poor tools to work with, or a good attitude but overwhelming customer demands, or a good attitude but no machinery, equipment, or fuel.

Attitude Seems to Outweigh Facts

Behavioral psychologists place more emphasis on attitude than on facts of the situation. Consider the story of the man who took his dog for a ride in his car.

Shortly before returning home, he stopped at the corner service station, which was located about 5 blocks from his home, to have his gas tank filled. While the tank was being filled, the man got out of his car to inspect the oil with the service station attendant. While waiting for the service station attendant to finish topping off the gas tank, the man began to tease the dog, who was still in the car with all the windows up, by running his hand around on the window. The dog stood up on the seat and began pawing on the window. In the process, the dog's paw hit the automatic door lock and locked all the car doors. Unfortunately, the car keys were still in the ignition.

The man decided to call his wife to bring her set of keys to salvage the situation. This she did, and they all went home.

That evening, the man, thinking it funny that the dog had locked him out of his car, recounted the story to a friend. The friend greeted the story with howls of laughter but, after regaining his composure, asked the man how he got the car open. He, of course, said that he had called his wife to bring down her set of keys, whereupon the friend said, "Boy, are you lazy."

The man's reply to that was, "Maybe I'm stupid because I let the dog lock me out of the car, but where do you get the idea that I'm lazy?"

The friend then said, "You were too lazy to walk the five blocks to your house and you made your wife bring you her keys."

"But you don't understand," the man said. "I certainly could have walked the entire distance, round trip to be sure, but my car was locked up at the service station pump; it was a busy time of day; I didn't want to just walk off and leave my car locked up at their pumps. And besides, I didn't know what the dog would do if I just left." To which the friend replied, "Well, hell, you could have taken the dog with you."

Needless to say, the friend had a difficult time explaining just *how* the man could have taken the dog with him.

The foregoing is an example of what happens when people get ideas in their minds about how things are and, frankly, don't want to be confused with facts. So what if the dog was locked in the car? The owner still could have taken the dog with him.

When people set out to prove something they have locked in their minds, they tend to argue from illogical positions.

Do You Want
a Good Attitude or the Desired Behavior?

Often you must decide whether you want a good attitude or the correct behavior. After all, we have no evidence that a good attitude necessarily brings desired behavior. To the contrary, examples of good attitude/poor behavior seem much more prevalent. For starters, consider a common moral problem. An awful lot of highly religious, devout people consider sinning bad. And they'll give testimonial to that on the Sabbath. But as any experienced preacher can tell you, between the periods when they attend to religious pursuits, many of the "true believers" don't behave the way they know they should.

And how many of us can relate to individuals who feel that losing a few pounds might be desirable, healthy and good for their little bodies? It is estimated that 40 percent of our population is on some kind of a diet at any given time. That's fine. Most of these dieters probably have a good attitude toward dieting. But do they have the correct behavior? Many medical doctors testify that starvation or fad diets actually do more harm than good to the human body. In the end, few dieters ever reach and maintain their desired weight.

How a Good Attitude Can Be Harmful

We have already seen that a good attitude does not necessarily produce the desired behavior. Let's take it one step further to see how a *good* attitude can actually produce harmful effects.

An employee with a "good attitude" volunteered to check on the boss's house while she was away on vacation. One day, driving by her house to "check things out" the employee saw two men carry a TV set out of a neighbor's house and put it in a van backed up in the neighbor's driveway.

The employee remembered his boss saying that her TV was not working and that she was having trouble arranging for someone to pick it up when she was home. Thus, the employee thought he could do a good turn, so he stopped to ask the TV repairmen to take his boss's TV into the shop for repairs along with the neighbor's. The TV repairmen immediately agreed to comply.

When the boss returned to work, she commended the subordinate on his thoughtfulness and initiative, and asked the neighbor which TV repair shop he used. Only then did she discover that the neighbor's house had been burglarized and that her TV set had been stolen along with the neighbor's property.

Do you still think it's attitude that counts?

Several years ago, I was traveling with a friend who was the president of a sizeable manufacturing operation. We were a little behind schedule on our way to catch a plane, but had ample time if all went right.

When we got to the airport, I told my friend to get the tickets and check the bags while I returned the rental car, thereby saving time. All went smoothly until I returned to the ticket counter where my friend was still in line, not yet having picked up the tickets, which were to be "ready for our immediate pick-up" upon arrival at the airport.

The problem was that the ticket agent was taking great pains to answer questions of travelers who seemingly had never flown before and who were ahead of my friend. The ticket agent droned on, manifesting his "good attitude" (and training, I might add), explaining in detail where they would be seated on the airplane, whether or not there would be meal service, whether or not they understood that they could not smoke in the "No Smoking" section, how to retrieve their bags when they arrived at their destination, etc. Well, my friend and I missed our flight because of this ticket agent's "good attitude."

Now, it is doubtless true that the ticket agent generated a lot of good will by being so reassuring and so thorough in his explanations to those inexperienced travelers. But he *did* lose the business of another customer who travels frequently and who personally bought several hundred dollars' worth of tickets each month. He actually lost the airline several *thousand* dollars per month, because my friend issued a mandate to all of his employees not to fly on this specific airline on company business if any alternative flights were available—if they did, they could expect not to be reimbursed for their airfare.

But the ticket agent still had a "good attitude." And some of those customers with whom he took a great deal of time to explain each detail will probably fly on that airline again—if they ever have occasion to fly again and if the airline happens to be flying where they want to go.

Furthermore, these occasional travelers, as is the case with most occasional travelers, were probably traveling on super-saver air fares for which they paid less than half the price for the same plane ride as my executive friend who was traveling first-class. Indeed, the airline probably lost more fare than it gained by boarding the new travelers and not boarding the company president and myself, forcing us to fly on a competing airline.

Examples of good attitude but wrong behavior are all over the place. Attitude simply is not that important in garnering good performance from an employee. Indeed, it's probably just as true that well-functioning employees may have bad attitudes, but engage in the correct behavior.

Besides, What Is a Good Attitude?

The foregoing, of course, emphasizes the fact that just because someone has a "good attitude" doesn't mean it will be constructive at work. It does *not* suggest that a bad attitude is desirable, and it does *not* negate the idea that a good attitude *may* be helpful *most* of the time.

But when we really get to the nitty-gritty, we need to consider what constitutes a good attitude. Practically always what is perceived as a good attitude in a subordinate is a viewpoint that coincides with the boss's viewpoint. Employees are often perceived as having a good attitude when they say, "Right, R.J.," or "You know, that's pretty much the way I was looking at it, too."

All of us are familiar with abrasive-type personalities. They are negative, veto-oriented people who question everything, challenge everything, never are willing to accept anything, and, frankly, are a pain in the behind. Abrasive personalities are always accused of having bad attitudes. Even when they are looked at kindly, they are usually viewed as being devil's advocates, but perhaps overly zealous in their advocacy. Also, according to Harry Levinson, they do not tend to get very high in the organization and practically never get to the top—because of their attitude.*

Quite honestly, defining the word "attitude" is extremely difficult for our purposes. It is based fundamentally upon judgment, and that judgment pretty much is a function of how one looks at things.

Attitude Just Isn't That Important

Ultimately, attitude really isn't very important when it comes to job performance. *Behavior* is what counts. And it really doesn't matter whether subordinates have good attitudes or bad attitudes so long as they get the job done and get the job done right, within legal, moral, and ethical constraints. In employees, attitude *isn't* the only thing that counts. It may help. But it isn't nearly as important as performance.

---

* Harry Levinson, "The Abrasive Personality," *Harvard Business Review*, (May–June 1978), pp. 86–94.

16

If You Can't Say
Anything Good About Someone,
Don't Say Anything at All

Most concerns about whether or not you should talk of others
if you can't say anything good are based on social graces, sen-
sitivity to other's egos, and whether someone's feelings might
get hurt.

Much "common managerial sense" grows out of the social
conventions and learning we experience as children. Therefore, most managers, bosses, and supervisors prefer to be "nice
guys"—or "gals"—and try to not say anything negative—partly out of fear that they might offend the subordinate or
associate, partly because of the fear that others won't think
kindly of them in their supervisory role.

How Will Employees Learn of Their Mistakes?

The idea behind the notion is decidedly good and kindly. If
you say only good things, you won't hurt people's feelings.
Furthermore, by being positive, you can be optimistic. But
when managers practice this, they soon find a significant problem beginning to occur. If the boss *never* criticizes someone's
poor, or erroneous, or inept performance, how will the unsatisfactory performers ever learn of their errors?

There are essentially two problems with a boss who is reluctant to point out unacceptable or inferior performance of a subordinate. One, of course, is that individuals are not made aware of their errors. The other is that employees are really being trained to perpetuate their errors.

The Case of the New Typist

As a graduate student at the University of Michigan, I was a teaching assistant in the College of Business. Being a teaching assistant, I would, on occasion, need secretarial help for such things as typing examinations, answering the telephone, and serving as a receptionist for students who had appointments with me.

However, when one is a teaching assistant, one isn't very high in the pecking order of status in a university. Consequently, the secretarial/typing help I received was a "share the wealth" situation—that is, there were several teaching assistants who had to share the services of one secretary. The sharing, however, posed no problem. None of us had that much work to do and certainly none of us required anything near a full-time assistant.

The problem was our typists. We always received new, inexperienced, or untrained typists. As our typists improved in their skills and other vacancies occurred, they moved up in the organizational hierarchy and became private secretaries, administrative assistants, or whatever was more suitable to their improved talents. Thus, we tended continuously to have the runt of the litter.

One of my colleagues was finishing his Ph.D. and was looking for a job as a professor at a major university. He not only required typing of exams and other teaching-assistant material, but also typing of letters to deans of other business schools around the country inquiring about possible positions. Thus, he was totally concerned about the quality of the typing that went into the final product.

When he started sending out his resumes and inquiring about job openings, we received a new typist. This typist was terrible, to make a modest understatement of the typist's ineptness. One of the letters, in alleged final form, contained no fewer than 13 uncorrected errors in a page and a half. Needless to say, my colleague was bitterly disappointed. So what did he do about it? He took it home to have his wife retype it!

Now, it would seem logical that someone smart enough to receive a Ph.D. in business would know a little bit more about the "common sense" of management. After all, management is just common sense—isn't it? But this same practice is seen over and over again in many offices. It is not at all unusual for bosses to take unsatisfactory work from a new employee and redo it themselves or give it to a more qualified employee to redo. They thereby accomplish two things: They fail to inform the employee of what was wrong with what he or she did, and they punish the other employee (or themselves) for the inept performer's poor work.

Is there any alternative to saying something critical about someone's work? Of course there is. You can try to be constructive and offer suggestions as to how the employee can improve. Most employees who are starting out are willing to accept the fact that they're not always knowledgeable about what is expected, and they usually appreciate help they are given. However, if uncorrected, at some point in time they begin to think they are doing the job acceptably well—and then they begin to get sensitive to "criticism." Yet, correcting the individual is the only way you can avoid punishing others for someone else's less-than-satisfactory work.

Being Trained to Perpetuate Poor Performance

A second problem with avoiding criticizing a subordinate's performance is that the individual is apt to get the idea that his or her performance is more than acceptable. For example, the typist in the grad school office went home that evening (after giving a letter to the boss with 13 uncorrected errors) with the idea that she must have done an acceptable job because "After all, nobody said there was anything wrong with it." She was probably not even aware that the letter contained any errors because no one mentioned it, and what kind of a boss would accept a letter with 13 errors?

The facts of the matter are that unless someone is willing to correct ineptness, ineptness will persist. This is true whether you're coaching a professional athletic team, helping someone get started in an avocation, or bossing an employee at work. Whenever a boss interacts with a subordinate, a degree of training is transpiring. If we do a job in some shoddy or unacceptable way and that work is accepted with nothing ever said about it, we begin to think that that's the standard and that it's acceptable. This is probably the single biggest reason that truly superior performance is seldom found in any organization. Bosses don't like to nag, bosses don't like to correct, bosses would just as soon not have to be negative; so they are often willing to accept mediocre performance of a subacceptable level.

The Major Problem of Not Being Critical

Probably the biggest problem of not being critical of an employee's performance comes from the term "past practices" or "precedent."

Anyone who has ever been involved in union/management relations knows well what these terms mean. If the union and management disagree, the union will argue "past practices" or "precedents," and the company will probably lose.

If the union can establish that the performance or behavior of an employee in *past practices* or in *precedental cases* has been acceptable, the arbitrators will decide that the company's behavior has led the employee to believe that what he or she was doing *unacceptably* well *is* actually acceptable. Therefore, no disciplinary or corrective punishment can be applied to that individual.

Companies can try to improve things *from that day forward*. They can do so by pointing out to the employee what is unacceptable performance or behavior. But they cannot discipline or reprimand the employee for prior sins because, according to the arbitrator, they are the ones who have encouraged the employee to believe that what he or she did was just fine.

They'll Probably Bad-Mouth You Anyway

Another consideration is the motive behind the lack of criticism. Many people, for political reasons, don't like to say anything negative about others because they don't want the "bad vibrations" getting fed back to the individual being disparaged. They certainly want to avoid saying anything libelous or slanderous, and they often hope that if they practice the Golden Rule (see Chapter 6), the adversary will probably not say anything negative about them, and everyone will be happy.

Nothing is likely to be further from the truth. As described in Chapter 6, the Golden Rule is inappropriate in supervisory practice for a variety of reasons. But even more importantly, as described in Chapter 8, when considering negotiation skills, you're probably better off taking a strong win–lose position than attempting to take an ameliatory position.

It is simply bad advice to assume that others are necessarily going to play by all the correct win–win rules. You'd have to get ten out of ten assumptions about your adversary correct *and* your adversary would have to have the same correct ten out of ten assumptions about you. The conclusion was that that is highly unlikely to happen very often.

You Trained Him, You Keep Him

Very few managers ever fire subordinates. Indeed, the lack of firing in U.S. business and industry has been well documented.* The probability of someone getting fired in a business is extremely remote (in contrast to their being "dehired," which is the subtle practice of trying to encourage people to quit).

If dehiring doesn't work, then bosses have very limited alternatives with employees who aren't doing a good job. The usual choices are such things as demoting them (again, rarely done), promoting them (the most commonly used practice), outplacing them (usually only done with top level executives), or getting the problem employee to take an early retirement (about as tricky as pulling off a dehiring).

---

* Lawrence L. Steinmetz, *Managing the Marginal and Unsatisfactory Performer* (Reading, Mass.: Addison-Wesley, 1969).

If all of the above fail, the only alternative left is to *transfer* the employee. Get someone else to take him or her off your hands. This is facilitated if the performance appraisals and reviews cite *good* things about the employee. This helps present a pretty good package to a fellow boss somewhere else in the organization—if that fellow boss is pretty naive.

But There Is a Fly in the Ointment

There's just one problem with the transferring tactic. It's so commonly used and so commonly known most supervisors who've had more than one lap around the track are totally aware of the different kinds of words and phraseology used in the "honest" performance reviews of good performers and the "glowing" evaluations of turkeys. Somehow the crackerjack performers of sterling quality have their performance adequately documented with *specific* examples of highly satisfactory performance. But those employees who are simply given a whitewash never have specific examples, never have documentation of instances where they pulled off anything tangible, always seem to have been "assisting," "helping," "involved," or "instrumental." They were never "in charge of," "responsible for." And anyone who knows how to read a performance review quickly ferrets out the wheat from the chaff.

So what happens if you've been saying good things about your employee, both to the employee's face and in writing? It keeps you from having to confront the subordinate. It keeps you from having to document inadequacy. It keeps you from having to say anything bad about anyone. It keeps you from hurting someone's feelings.

And it also keeps the employee with you, because you aren't going to be able to pull off a transfer. And after having said all those good things, you won't be able to fire the employee. And if he or she's been doing such a good job, it will be tough talking him or her into retiring. And you sure as hell can't demote someone who's been doing such a good job. So maybe the only thing you can do is put him or her in for a promotion. So now we know why so many people get promoted when they are doing an unsatisfactory job. It doesn't just happen to football coaches. There are an awful lot of *de facto* athletic directors in business and industry.

If You Want to Manage, You've Got to Tell the Truth

So what's the long and short of the idea that as a supervisor you should never say anything negative about anyone? The facts are that if you don't, you're never going to teach them the error of their ways. If you don't you'll get them to think that they've been doing a good job. If you don't, you'll train them to continue to do poor work because it is the perceived acceptable standard. If you don't, you may have a serious ''past practices'' or ''precedental'' problem. If you never engage in constructive criticism, your employees will probably *not* respect or appreciate the fact that you simply haven't said anything negative. They will just think they are perfect. And your reward for this accomplishment is that you'll probably get to keep the turkey as your number-one assistant for years to come.

17

People Rise to Their Level of Incompetence

Lawrence J. Peter years ago wrote a book called *The Peter Principle*. Essentially, Peter's principle states that employees rise to their own level of incompetence.

This idea at first took the nation by storm. Everyone knew someone who was incompetent in his or her position and that in itself seemed to prove that people rise to a level of incompetence. After all, the people being perceived as incompetent had been promoted there.

What Does It Mean To Rise to a Level of Incompetence?

Imagine that a top-level producer, because of her outstanding job performance, is promoted to a higher level position (virtually always a supervisory position) only to become incompetent—because she can't manage effectively or hasn't been trained to cope with the problems supervisors must face (or because she just lacks talent).

If the person is *successful* at the job to which she rose, according to Peter's principle, she will *again* be promoted, at which time she *again* may become incompetent (or may be successful, in which case she is again promoted). Presumably, however, at some point the person will rise to a position where she is no longer competent, for whatever reason. Then this person becomes a shelf-sitter and we have a classic example of Peter's principle.

The logic behind Peter's principle is virtually impeccable. It is painfully obvious that all people sooner or later top out in some position. Or at least most all people should. But do they really?

Why People Fail to Perform

The Peter Principle states that when people fail to perform competently at their jobs, it is because they are unable to perform effectively. But there are really only three reasons why people don't perform effectively at their jobs, only one of which is lack of competence. Those three reasons are (1) they can't do the job, (2) they won't do the job, or (3) they don't know to do the job.

Those Who Can't Do the Job

Many people fail at performing their jobs because they *can't* do them. That is, they get put into a position where they are inept at doing the job, so they do it unsatisfactorily or unacceptably. This is really the situation that Peter's principle describes.

There are several reasons why people *can't* do a job. They don't know *how* to do the job, they don't have the *resources* with which to do the job, or someone or something is *interfering* with their ability to do the job.

Lack of training. The classic reason why people rise to a level of incompetence is that they *can't* do the job *because they don't know how.*

When people don't know how to do a job, it invariably is because they have not been taught how to do it. A person cannot fly an airplane because she has not been *taught* to fly an airplane. Therefore, if this person is promoted to company pilot to fly the company aircraft, she will likely fail. She has therefore risen to a level of incompetence. She *can't* do the job.

But whose fault is that? Obviously if she were trained she could do the job, so it really isn't the employee's fault that she *can't* (or doesn't) succeed as company pilot. It's because she was *not given* adequate training by her employer.

Lack of resources. A second reason why people really can't do a job is not having adequate tools or materials. Let's say our pilot has her pilot's license and is more than adequately trained to fly the type aircraft our company owns. Now she surely can fly the airplane. So we ask her to fly us from Denver to Albuquerque. We climb into the corporate jet and she says, "We'll have to get some fuel, at least enough to fly to Albuquerque." However, because of the fuel shortage, no one will sell us jet fuel. Again, our pilot will fail. We won't get to Albuquerque because she is unable to fly the plane—not because she doesn't know how, but because *she doesn't have the resources*—in this case the fuel to do the job.

In many cases, people are unable to perform their jobs competently because of lack of resources. Executives often fail because they don't have a sufficient number of employees. This is equally true of the typist who fails because there is no typewriter, and the military commander who fails because the supply lines don't supply the combat materials or because there are not enough troops. Is the military commander incompetent? the typist? the pilot? Hardly. Yet people who fail because of lack of resources are usually perceived as incompetent. It takes a mighty lucky person to be perceived as not being incompetent when, indeed, lack of resources is the cause.

Task interference problem. Let's say we hire a pilot who is adequately licensed and trained to fly our aircraft, and we have abundant fuel. So now we say to her, "Let's fly to Albuquerque." We get in and get ready to take off and she dutifully calls the control tower for clearance for taking off. The air traffic controller says to our pilot, however, that permission is denied because of bad weather conditions. Our pilot has failed again! Again she may be alleged to be incompetent. Doesn't she know how to fly in inclement weather? Of course she does. We said she was duly qualified to fly, and in a corporate jet like ours this would mean instrument flight qualifications as well as visual qualifications. But whose fault is it that she failed? In this case, it's the heavens above. But the pilot might be blamed for it.

I Didn't Know You Wanted Me To

Yet another reason that people often fail and are perceived as incompetent is because they *don't know to do the job*. This is not really the fault of the individual employee and does not prove that he or she is incompetent. After all, he simply didn't know what he was supposed to do. In essence, the "don't-know-to-do" situation is the result of a communications breakdown. If a middle-level manager is not told what the job entails or what various job requirements may be, that manager may not do something necessary for successful achievement of his or her job.

Now, to be sure, many times people argue that they fail because they didn't know to do something when in fact they *did* know. Usually they offer excuses like "I didn't know" to alleviate the blame for their ineptitude.

Consider the individual who has been stopped by a highway patrol officer and who is about to receive a citation for his or her driving skills. Usually the conversation goes something like this:

> Patrol officer: "Do you know how fast you were going?"
> Motorist: "No, sir."
> Patrol officer: "I clocked you at 75 miles per hour."
> Motorist: "Is that right? Golly, I sure didn't know that. I had no idea I was going anywhere near that fast. Are you sure? I certainly wouldn't have been driving that fast had I known I was going that fast."
> Patrol officer: "Do you know what the speed limit is here on Interstate 40?"
> Motorist: "Uuh, no."
> Patrol officer: "It's 55 miles per hour."
> Motorist: "Is that right? Golly, I didn't know that. I thought out here in the West the speed limits were higher. When did they post the speed limits at 55 miles per hour? Gosh, you know, I surely wouldn't have been going in excess of 55 miles per hour if I had known the speed limit was only 55 miles per hour."

Most all of us have gone through a similar drill—not necessarily in getting a speeding ticket, but perhaps when having gotten caught off base for some relatively minor violation, such as parking in a No Parking zone, going the wrong way in a one-way alley, bumping a meal line, or engaging in other nefarious pursuits. "Gosh, I'm sorry, I didn't realize..." are not unknown words to most of our population.

I Won't Do the Job

The third reason why people fail to perform effectively on the job is because they don't *want* to do the job. This is an attitudinal problem. It's part and parcel of the deceitful side of saying "I didn't know to do," but it is much more obvious.

If it is justifiable to say that someone rose to a level of incompetence, it is most justifiable when the reason he or she is not successful is because he or she doesn't want to be. This may mean that he or she is not adequately motivated—but whatever the derivative cause of the lack of motivation, the person is now in a position of incompetence, but for attitudinal reasons.

Usually the Job Outgrows the Person or the Person Burns Out

The truth of the matter is that very seldom do people rise to a level of incompetence in an organization. Practically always they get into a job and handle it just fine. That is because they can do it, they want to do it, and they know how to do it.

Also, given the quality of training that most organizations give their personnel, most people who are put into jobs *are* trained, *are* given adequate tools and resources with which to do the job, *have* interferences removed, *are* adequately appraised as to what needs to be done and, assuming they *want* to do the job, *do* the job successfully.

When people do *not* perform well in a job, it's not because they have been promoted *to* a job, but because they've been in a job so long that they've let the job *outgrow* them or, in today's vernacular, they experience "job burn-out."

Job Burn-out

It has become vogue to say you're getting "burned out" on the job. This, of course, is just a convenient buzz word to use to publicly announce that you're no longer motivated to do your job and that you don't want to feel bad about it. So you explain that you've simply burned out, you're no longer motivated. This is an admission upon your part that you *won't* do the job. It probably also implies that you are incompetent by your own volition and, therefore, have risen to a level of incompetence more or less coincidentally with experiencing burn-out. Extrapolating from Daniel Levinson's and Homer R. Figler's* books, this may be more a function of the seasons of a person's life than a lack of competency.

The Job Just Gets Bigger Than the Person

Most commonly, then, when someone is truly found incompetent in his job, the job has outgrown him. It is one thing for an individual to be Vice President of Production in a small manufacturing company employing a total of 17 persons, of which 12 are direct-line production employees. In this case, the Vice President of Production is really nothing more than a production expediter.

But what happens if that small company grows to 200 or 300 employees? Still not a giant organization by standards of our industrial giants, but a behemoth compared to the 17-person organization. As is usually the case, the Vice President of Production is still Vice President of Production. But now the Vice President of Production needs to be a true manager of the production process rather than an expediter— and this is when the job outgrows the individual.

This phenomenon can be observed commonly in small businesses. The same phenomenon is not so easily observed in larger businesses but is every bit as much there.

---

* Daniel J. Levinson, *The Seasons of a Man's Life* (New York: Ballantine, 1978), and Homer R. Figler, *Overcoming Executive Midlife Crisis* (New York: Wiley, 1978).

Technical Competence Doesn't Get People Fired

According to a study published in 1978 by George S. Odiorne,* there are 14 reasons why managers get fired. As he points out in the George Odiorne Letter, "Though managers are hired for technical knowledge, this isn't among the 14 reasons why managers fail and end up being fired."

The 14 categories of reasons why managers fail all relate to how the executives got along in the organization. As Odiorne points out:

No managers were fired for lack of technical knowledge.

No managers were fired for taking too many chances on innovations.

No managers were fired because of deficiencies in their educational background.

The reasons they *were* fired are as follows:

1. Couldn't control emotions.
2. Behaved immaturely.
3. Lacked a sense of urgency.
4. Let trivial obstacles stop him/her.
5. Couldn't respond to change quickly enough.
6. Hung on to obsolete ways of doing things.
7. Evidenced hostility to the organization.
8. Persistently tore up employee relations by his/her supervisory behavior.
9. Didn't know when to stick rigidly to policy and when to deviate from it.
10. Couldn't delegate or wouldn't ask for help.
11. Couldn't communicate, write, speak, or listen effectively.
12. Wasn't tough enough.
13. Lacked a sense of timing.
14. Seldom or never anticipated what lay ahead.

Managers get fired because they lose political favor, they don't have the motivation, emotional strength, or courage to do the job, or they have personality or emotional problems.

---

* "Executive Effectiveness," *The George Odiorne Letter* (October 1978), No. 5.

So another truth bites the dust. It's unfortunate, too. Most of us like to believe that people rise to a level of incompetence. This gives some vindictive hope for the future when we see some "unworthy" person getting a promotion that we didn't get. We can soothe our feelings with the idea that sooner or later this nonmeritorious person will top out and fail. The truth is they will probably top out because of lack of motivation. Or the job may outgrow them. But they are not likely to top out because they are incapable of handling their jobs.

18

Blackmail is Bad— and So Is Bribery

This chapter is probably misnamed. It's not really about blackmail, and it's not really about bribery. What it's really about is positive reinforcement—and whether or not positive reinforcement is as good a motivator as it's cracked up to be.

Positive Reinforcement

It has become very popular among management experts to discuss behavior modification (see Chapter 15), which incorporates the principles of positive and negative reinforcement.

According to *Business Week* magazine, positive reinforcement and behavior modification are really hot stuff in U.S. business and industry.* They state that

When Edward J. Feeney pioneered the systematic use of "positive reinforcement" to cut costs by $2 million a year at Emery Air Freight Corporation a decade ago, few in the mainstream of management innovation paid much attention.... Now, though still in an evolutionary stage in business, the Feeney techniques, commonly called "behavior modification" and identified with Harvard psychologist B.F. Skinner,

---

* Productivity Gains from a Pat on the Back," *Business Week*, (January 23, 1978), pp. 56, 58, 62.

are increasingly being recognized as a valuable tool with which managers can combat slumping productivity growth rates, reduce absenteeism and turnover, and, in most cases, provide increased job satisfaction for employees.

Like many truths, positive reinforcement sounds good. It's a nice, easy, comfortable thing to do. The boss can be a "nice guy" or "gal" again. Everybody likes to hand out little rewards for jobs well done.

But Isn't It Bribery?

The problem with positive reinforcement is that it is tantamount to bribery. And we all say that bribery, like blackmail, is bad. But maybe it's good if it gets the workers to do what bosses want them to do, easily, without much strain.

Operant Conditioning

Positive reinforcement theory states that when someone does something we want them to do, we want them to continue to do, and we want them to have a good attitude about doing, we should give them "positive reinforcement"—or rewards—for doing such good things.

If you want a dog to learn how to shake hands, you take it through the motions and then reward it with a biscuit, and the dog presumably is motivated to do it again to get another biscuit. Then, when the dog does it again, it is again rewarded. After several tries, the dog figures out that by extending its paw to shake hands, it can get a biscuit. Finally it learns that when you say "Shake," it should extend its paw because that's what you want it to do. And it may (or may not) get a biscuit. And the dog is ultimately satisfied to do that whether or not it gets a biscuit—because usually it will get some kind of reward, anyhow.

So positive reinforcement essentially boils down to animal training. Indeed, this is why Nicholas Von Hoffman, in his article about positive reinforcement and behavior modification, referred to B.F. Skinner as a "Harvard rat psychologist."* In Von Hoffman's words, B.F. Skinner teaches that "Just as you can make rodents perform in certain ways by rewarding and punishing them, you can work your will on human beings in similar fashion."

But can behavior modification really be applied to human beings at work? And is it really an ethical practice?

Can It Be Applied at Work?

Positive reinforcement systems at work are awfully hard to find in the United States. Time was there were many programs, but they seemed to die out. Company executives testify that *if* they use it, they feel it is very expensive. It's also only a break-even as to whether or not it's worth the effort, time, and money that must be put into it to achieve success at "combatting slumping productivity growth rates, reducing absenteeism and turnover, and, in most cases, providing increased job satisfaction for employees."** Most executives are unhappy not so much because it is impossible to employ, but because it is essentially *not worth it*. And many of them feel that not only is it not worth it, but it may ultimately be an undesirable practice on moralistic grounds.

Bribery and Positive Reinforcement

Rewards at work take many forms. It may be a pat on the head, but very commonly it's something tangible—A 10 cent an hour bonus, a ham or a turkey, or a case of beer.

Why is it a bonus or a ham? Because a pat on the head has been used for years and hasn't proved all that productive. Something tangible has to be there to keep interest in a work program. Furthermore, the tangible reward had better be

---

* Nicholas Von Hoffman, "A Choice Between 'Behavior Modification' and Cattle Prods." *The Rocky Mountain News*, January 31, 1978, p. 33.

** "Productivity," loc. cit.

changed regularly, like menus in a prison or a college dorm. It's the principle of the Hawthorne effect (see Chapter 9) all over again. After all, one might be motivated for a week or two to try to win a ham or a turkey and then get tired of eating ham or turkey. So then it better be a fifth of whiskey, 5 gallons of gas, or an ice chest. Because you can only accept so many hams for doing well, or you start oinking.

Yet It Is Still Bribery

But bribery is still the primary philosophical disagreement that plagues positive reinforcement schemes and the implementation of behavior modification practices. The reason is that workers are *paid* to do their job, and any rewards they get from behavior modification/positive reinforcement principles are *something extra*. That is, a worker is paid to come to work and do a job. But if that worker isn't highly motivated, then the company employs positive reinforcement principles and opts to give the employee *extra* rewards, above and beyond those agreed to, for doing work for which the employee is *already being paid*. That's where the bribery aspect shows up.

Just because someone comes to work on time—or comes to work at all and thereby ''reduces absenteeism''—why should he or she receive an *extra* reward? After all, employees are supposed to come to work on a regular basis. And they are not supposed to come to work late. And they are supposedly motivated to maintain a basic level of productivity. So when something *extra* is provided those employees, it is frequently viewed as bribery—at least by those who provide the ''something extra.'' And the problem with bribery is that the person who *accepts* the bribe usually becomes contemptuous of the giver. And then the system begins to fall apart.

I'll Give You Ten Bucks for Every ''A'' You Get

What's the difference between an incentive on the one hand and bribery on the other? Incentives are paid as an ''incentive bonus'' to a production employee or as a commission to a sales person for going out and beating the bushes and doing a great job. But we call it bribery when we ask an invoice clerk who works for a competitor to supply us with the competitor's customer list, or when we ask a person who has just quit the employment of a competitor to give us a list of names of customer prospects for the competitor. In both cases we're asking the recipient to do a job. The only difference is that in the one case it is considered ethical and in the other it is not considered ethical.

Legality also enters into the question. Bribery is illegal, but offering incentive programs is not illegal. But if that is the fine line of distinction, answer the following.

Let's Go See a Show

Anyone who's ever gone to Las Vegas to take in a show may have a difficult time differentiating between "bribery" and "incentive." One can get a reservation for a table or seat to see one's favorite entertainer simply by calling in, making a reservation, getting there early, standing in line, and finally being seated.

But many people learn that if one doesn't like one's seat and/or if one doesn't wish to stand in line, and/or if one doesn't even wish to call in a reservation, one can probably get a seat *anyway.* This is done by the process of tipping. Is a tip a bribe? Is a tip an incentive? If you've ever felt that you *had* to tip in order to be seated at all, you have probably felt it was bribery. But it is perfectly legal. Or at least it doesn't seem to be an activity that any of the legal beagles in Nevada are concerned about eliminating or correcting.

Many people feel tipping is tantamount to bribery. Many people also resent the recipient of the bribe/tip. This is much the same reaction that many companies who have administered positive reinforcement systems seem to have developed after having to bribe/motivate employees to do a job for which they were *already* supposedly adequately compensated.

So Is Positive Reinforcement a Fundamental Management Truth?

Again, when we check out positive reinforcement as a motivational device, we begin to question its validity. The truth seems pure; the idea behind it seems feasible; it has a good ring to it. But like many things in practice, it seems to deteriorate. King Arthur's Round Table sounded good, too. But it fell to the foibles of humanity. Many of the other truths we now know—and probably others we will discover in the future—will meet the same demise.

V

Truth in Selling

19

The Best Way
to Motivate a Salesperson
Is To Pay Commission

At a recent seminar in Milwaukee, several top-level executives were discussing ways to enhance and promote sales volume in their organizations. One of them indicated that the single best way to motivate salespeople is to pay by commission. Several other executives in the group nodded in knowing agreement. Only a few didn't get too excited.

Why Commission Salespeople Are Motivated

There are a variety of ways to motivate people: Some people are motivated by money, others by power, yet others by fear or greed, and some even by a desire to serve the human race. But one thing that is for sure is that salespeople, as a group, seem to be primarily motivated by possessions and things, which essentially comes down to making a big buck. Therefore, the best motivator for salespeople *should* be a high commission.

Some executives disagree with this idea. They argue that indeed, to the contrary, salespeople are *not* motivated to work as effectively as they might if they were *not* paid strictly by commission. Why is there disagreement?

The logic behind paying commission is that people are motivated to sell more, because the more they sell, the more money they make. Furthermore, they are motivated to sell at a high price, because then, again, they get more. Thus, the magic scheme for motivation, doubly valuable because of its simplicity, is to pay sales reps a straight commission on their sales. They don't get paid if they don't work. They make more if they sell more and at a higher price.

I Want a Piece of the Action

It's difficult to find a sales representative who doesn't seem to want a piece of the action. As they explain it, their direct participation in the company benefits realized from the fruits of their own labors motivates them to work diligently and produce results. Therefore, "Pay me by commission. Give me a commission against how much I sell. If I don't sell anything, I don't get paid. So you're guaranteed that I'll do a good job, etc., etc." This is repeated time and time again by salespeople explaining the simplicity and laudable nature of their motivation. Keep it simple: "If I do a good job, I make a lot; if I don't, I won't. If I'm making money, you're making money. If you're not making any money, I'm not."

So everyone at least claims to want a piece of the action. But do they really? And what do they mean by a "piece of the action"? It is true that if they don't sell anything they don't make anything—but while they are not *making* anything, the company is probably *losing* something.

When salespeople do nothing, nothing much happens for them. They don't make any money—but they don't have to work. They can go play golf. But when salespeople do not sell anything, something *does* happen to the company. Fixed costs march on. Plant overhead prevails. Interest charges at the bank on raw materials, work in process, and finished goods inventory continues to be charged. Office overhead personnel continue to collect their salaries. Office machinery and equipment stand expensively idle. Land and building costs carry on. Charges for machinery and equipment not being used continue to be logged. In short, all of the fixed daily operations of the business continue, whether the sales rep is playing golf or out beating the bushes. So it's not true at all that nothing happens if the salespeople don't produce sales: nothing happens for the sales rep, but the company begins to lose money.

So what do sales reps really mean by wanting a "piece of the action"—by being paid a commission? It indicates that they don't understand at all what a "piece of the action" means—or *they understand altogether too well* that a "piece of the action" means *profiting* when the other profits and *losing* when the other loses, but they figure the employer is too dumb (or too weak) to insist on it being a two-way street. Very few sales reps are willing to dig into their own pockets to fund the company losses on a pro-rata basis when the company is unprofitable because of no sales.

But the truth is that a "piece of the action" means participating fully and completely *whichever way* the action goes. A piece of the action does not mean profit sharing (a concept that many alleged dynamic sales reps will talk). A piece of the action means profit *and loss* sharing—a concept most sales reps shun almost as exclusively as they shun skunk oil. Most salespeople may think that a piece of the action should be a one-way street—if the company sells a product and they're involved in the sale, they want a piece of the gross—but they don't want a piece of the loss, which might be incurred if they are not selling and the company is not profiting.

The Fundamental Problem with Commission Sales Plans

The fundamental problem with commission sales payments is that they do not motivate the salesperson to work for the company he or she represents. Commission sales schemes motivate the sales reps to work *for the customers*. By their training and intuition, sales reps already work for their customers: The problem is compounded by the fact that earning a small commission on a low *selling* price is far better than earning no commission on a high *asking* price. Furthermore, it is a good deal easier to *write orders* for products that are virtually running out the manufacturer's door than to *sell* a customer on buying products from the manufacturer. Finally, selling skills do require some work, and the truth of the matter is, some sales reps are not particularly interested in working very hard.

Sales Reps Work for Customers

Sales reps are taught that if they are to be effective they must look at their product or service from the customer's point of view. They should *identify* with the customer. They should *understand* the customer's uses, needs, and applications for the product they're selling. The better they know the customer's needs, the better they will be able to sell the product.

Any basic sales training program incorporates the fundamental ideas of the FAB technique. FAB is an acronym for "features, advantages, and benefits." (Features explain details about the product. Advantages explain how these features work. Benefits explain how the customer will *benefit* from *using* the product.) Sales reps are taught to emphasize benefits the customer will derive from the use of the product—not the features or advantages of the product itself. If the rep understands how the customer can best benefit from buying and using the product, the rep will be more effective at selling it to the customer.

Consider a sales rep selling a cordless electric drill. A feature of that cordless electric drill is that it's cordless. But being cordless doesn't mean anything; it simply is a statement of fact. The customer presumably will not see any advantage in its being cordless or any benefit in the fact that the electric drill is without a cord.

One advantage of a cordless electric drill is that it doesn't weigh as much. Another is that there's no cord to get tangled in. Other advantages might include the fact that the cordless electric drill does not take up as much space and is not apt to get caught (the cord, that is) in one's bicycle spokes (should one be riding around on a bike with a cordless electric drill in hand). And on and on go the advantages of the cordless electric drill.

But what the customers are presumably interested in is, what can the cordless electric drill do for them? This is the fundamental question all buyers need to have answered before they will purchase any product or service. Therefore the sales rep is trained to think in terms of *benefits*, not features. "How will the customer benefit from purchasing our product?" is the all-important question the astute sales rep answers to earn that valuable "piece of the action."

The obvious benefits for a customer of a cordless electric drill are that (a) no electrical outlet is necessary to use the product, and (b) it is lighter in weight and therefore less fatiguing to use.

As an additional example, why would you buy a stainless steel sink rather than a porcelain sink? Because of the features? You just want stainless steel rather than porcelain? Probably not. Because of advantages? Stainless steel is lighter and stronger? Probably not. Most people don't carry sinks around with them. The reason you might buy a stainless steel sink rather than a porcelain sink is because of the benefits which the features and advantages of stainless steel have over porcelain. Stainless steel does not stain; therefore it is easily cleaned. The ease of cleaning is the benefit to the user. Furthermore, stainless steel doesn't crack or chip (porcelain does), which will give a more pleasing, aesthetic, and long-lasting life to the sink. "Now I see why I want to buy a stainless steel sink. It will make my housekeeping chores easier and my house appear less beat up. Thank you for explaining to me the benefits I will realize from installing a stainless steel sink in my home rather than a porcelain sink," thinks the customer.

Price Is a Feature

Any good sales training program will also teach the sales rep that price is a feature—not a benefit—of the product. Any product has a price—it may be low or high—but it has a price. Good sales reps are taught to minimize price comparison, because *price is a feature.* "This drill is $49.95 and that drill is $39.95, so let's not talk about the feature of the product, let's talk about how it will benefit you. This product will punch a hole in the wall for you in your attic without dragging a long extension cord through the house. That product won't. That's why you want to buy this $49.95 electric cordless drill rather than the $39.95 drill, which requires a cumbersome and expensive $15.00 extension cord to go with it to punch the hole in the attic where you want to punch it."

Good sales reps are told to discuss *benefits*. This, they are advised, will overcome price objections. But the long and short of it is that price *is* a feature by which all products can be compared. "This one is cheaper than that one and I can punch a hole in my attic with either of them. So why shouldn't I buy the cheaper one?" asks the purchaser. "If I buy the cheaper one I will save $10.00. And I already have a $15.00 extension cord that I can drag up to the attic and use with the standard electric drill."

Meeting price resistance is a problem for most sales reps. Invariably customers argue down the benefits for the higher priced model. They say they will buy the higher priced cordless model only if the price is "competitive" with the lower priced cord-requiring model. So the sales rep, in trying both to please and to convince the customer to buy, has an enormous amount of pressure to quote a lower price. And that's where problem number two enters into the case *against* motivating sales people by paying them strictly by commission.

Something Beats Nothing All to Hell

When a sales rep is faced by a buyer who's shopping primarily on the basis of price, the commissioned salesperson has to face one unalterable fact: If a sale is made, the rep will get 7 percent of the selling price; if the sale is not made, the rep will get 7 percent of nothing. Therefore, selling a product at *any* price gets some return on the rep's time invested in closing the sale. So, under the idea that something beats nothing all to hell, the sales rep has a tremendous motivation to meet the competitor's price.

If reps have the prerogative of cutting prices, they are highly motivated to do so. Seven percent of a $40 sale is $2.80. Seven percent of a $50 sale that is not consummated is zero. Far better to get $2.80 return on one's time invested in selling than to get nothing returned on that same time invested in the selling effort because one hangs tight on (what now appears to be) too high a price.

So the sales rep becomes motivated to go to the sales manager and say, "Our price is too high. The customer won't buy. Our competition is cutting our price. There's no demand for our product at that price. You can't sell anything that's this overpriced. Our competition is beating our pants off.''

One fundamental problem with paying people strictly on commission against sales is that there is an enormously strong motivation for them to be the price cutter, to understand how the customer looks at it, to be competitive, to have a product that will "really move" in the marketplace.

This all argues that the salespeople do *not* work for the company they are representing; the salespeople work for the customer to whom they are selling. And this will always be true whenever the sales rep has any authority to do any price negotiating or price cutting. In fact, the only time that paying a sales rep strictly on commission against sales makes any sense at all is when the sales rep has *no authority whatsoever*, under any conditions, to change the selling price of the product—which would include also not having the authority to badger the sales manager or pricing specialist who determines the price to be charged for the product.

It's Easier To Write Orders Than It Is To Sell

Some sales reps are just order takers; other sales reps actually try to sell products. But you can pretty well be assured that the easier the product is to sell, the more of it will be sold. And one thing that is almost inevitably true (but not always—see Chapter 21) is that the lower the price on the product, the easier it is to sell.

Many astute sales managers and sales executives have observed that when they use a manufacturing rep organization to sell their company's products, the manufacturer's reps stumble all over themselves when "it looks like something I can sell." And any product of this nature has certain attributes to it. Number one, there is a high commission to the manufacturer's rep. Number two, the selling price is low, or perceived as low, by the manufacturer's rep relative to the competitive products. Number three, there is a very strong demand built up for the product because of the advertising already done by the manufacturer or because of lack of availability of supply of competitive products.

In short, manufacturer's reps evaluate representing certain products they sell largely on the basis of how easily they can be sold. It boils down to, "Will the telephone ring so that I can write up orders that I can forward to the manufacturer on which I can collect my commission? Or will I actually have to get out and shake the bushes, make calls on customers, spend a lot of time on the road, make a lot of sales presentations, drag around a lot of catalogs and demonstrators and, in short, work?"

There is no motivation for the sales rep to charge a high price. In fact, the lower the price, the better, because of the higher demand. And it doesn't take an astute mathematician to figure out that if you get 7 percent of $10,000 you make $700 for writing up orders on a low-priced, easily sold product. But if you can only sell $1,000 worth of the product—and make more calls and pound the bushes harder—you still make only $70 commission and have worked a lot harder in trying to generate that income. "Don't bring me a product that isn't appropriately (that is, low) priced. And don't lock me into a price. Because prices have to be negotiated. Prices need to be realistic," is the rep's argument. Indeed, one certain indicator that a product's price is too low is when the sales reps *quit* complaining that the price is too high.

We Need Something I Can Sell

Several years ago, on a consulting assignment in the Pacific Northwest, I was working with a retail client who was in a seasonal business. At the close of the season there was a lot of unsold merchandise, and one of the partners of the business wanted to know if I thought it would be a good idea for them to open a second store. I asked this partner why he was interested in opening a second store, particularly in view of the fact that sales had been so dismal that season, and that there was so much unsold merchandise that would have to be carried over to next season, incurring interest charges and similar costs to the business.

This partner replied that, after all, what they needed to get into their main store was merchandise that would sell. Therefore, his idea was that they could open a second "discount" store, wherein they could blow out the inventory left over at the close of the last season's sales. At this point I explained that, indeed, the merchandise they could *sell* was still in their store. The merchandise that *sold itself* had already jumped off the counter and walked out of the door in the hands of buyers.

If something doesn't sell, it always seems the fault is in the product. But if something sells well, the sales reps credit their crackerjack sales ability.

So How Do You Motivate Sales Reps?

One way to motivate sales reps, of course, is to have a fixed price. If the reps cannot negotiate the price, and are paid only commission, they either sell at that price or they don't get paid. They are successful or unsuccessful.

But, as already pointed out, when the salesperson does nothing, the company actually *loses* money because of the ongoing operational costs. Also, it is often expedient in a competitive market to give sales reps the opportunity to negotiate price. Many buyers simply will not buy if the price is not negotiable. So how do you give your sales representatives the opportunity to negotiate price and still motivate them to sell at as high a price as possible? The answer is relatively simple, but many employers don't like to go to the bother of structuring a format that will motivate a sales representative to sell a lot in dollar volume at as high a price as can be extracted. It sounds too complicated. But all that is really required is an understanding of the interrelationship between selling price, maintained gross profit margin on the products sold, and the commission rate paid.

The Importance of Gross Profit

A salesperson's compensation should be tied to not only the dollar volume the rep is selling, but also to the gross profit dollars realized on the product sold at whatever price it is sold. Consider a simple example. Say someone sells a hundred purses for $10 each for a total sales volume of $1,000. If the manufacturer's cost for producing these purses was $7 each, then the total manufacturer's cost for producing these purses was $700 and the gross profit margin realized on the purses was $300.

Sales	$1000
Cost of goods sold	700
Gross profit margin	$ 300

Had the same sales representative sold the same number of purses for $11, then the total selling price would have been $1,100 and the gross profit margin would have been $400:

Sales	$1100
Cost of goods sold	700
Gross profit margin	$ 400

In the first case, the gross margin realized on the sale was 30 percent. In the second case, the gross margin realized on the sale was 36.3 percent. In this case, the company stands to make $100 more in gross profit dollars than it could in the first situation. This was accomplished by selling at a higher price—and it shows up in *gross* margin dollars.

In contrast, a sales rep might have sold the same hundred purses at $9 each. The total selling price will be $900 and the gross margin is $200.

Sales	$900
Cost of goods sold	700
Gross profit margin	$200

The gross profit margin percentage was only 22.2 percent. Now the company has a decidedly lesser opportunity to make a profit, considerably less than if the same unit of sales was made at the $10 per-purse or $11 per-purse price.

The accompanying graph represents possible monthly sales compensations to reps who sell 1,000 purses. One uses a selling price of $9 per purse, maintaining a gross profit margin of 22.2 percent; one sells at $10 per purse, maintaining a gross profit margin of 30 percent; and one uses $11 per purse, reflecting a gross profit margin of 36.3 percent. *In addition*, Figure 19–1 also shows the income earned by a sales rep who sold 1,500 purses at a selling price of $11 per purse, also maintaining a 36.3-percent gross profit margin. This person will obviously make the most money because he or she realized the most gross profit dollars for the company (the gross margin on the selling price was not only high, but the total dollars of sales

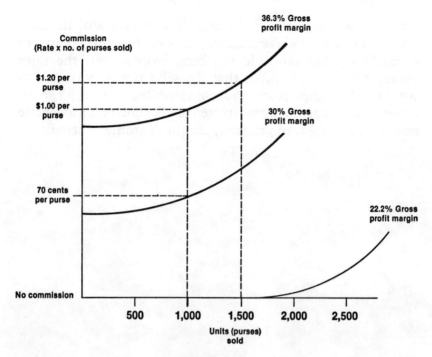

FIGURE 19-1

volume were also high). Thus, the sales rep who sold at the 22.2-percent gross profit margin will receive *no* commission—even though 1,000 units were sold—because the company will probably lose money on those sales. The rep who sold 1,000 units at 30-percent gross profit margin will receive $700 (1,000 units times 70 cents); the one who sold 1,000 units at 36.6-percent gross profit margin will make $1,080 ($1.08 times 1,000 units); and the one who sold 1,500 units at a gross profit margin of 36.3 percent will earn $1,800 (1,500 times $1.20 per purse). The higher commission *per unit* of sales at the 36.3-percent selling price is available to the rep who sold 1,500 units because the gross profit margin curve in Figure 19-1 slopes upward to the right to reward higher unit sales at any given gross profit percentage.

Making up schedules like this for compensating salespeople is relatively simple. It takes a little graph paper and a little time figuring out just exactly how much a certain sales volume at a certain gross margin is worth. But once established, it has the advantage of compensating the sales rep for what he or she does *for the company* in terms of the unit volume of sales made *and* dollar value of that unit volume of sales. Once this schedule has been worked out, the sales manager can be convinced that the sales rep is motivated to work *for the company* and to accomplish *the company's goals*, rather than simply being motivated to take orders at a low price and remain employed primarily for the customer's benefit.

20

Competition
Keeps Cutting My Price

Most sales representatives will argue that their competition always keeps cutting their price, and therefore it's difficult, if not impossible, to sell any product or service at a reasonable price.

This "truth" is really not a truth at all. In fact, it might be the least credible of all truths discussed in this book.

My Competition Is Reasonable

If salespeople feel that their competition is *not* cutting their price, it's *primarily* because the competition charges an even higher price than they do.

Whoever is the low-priced supplier in any field is *perceived* as the price cutter in the industry by those who charge higher prices. It is true that many people *want* to be—and try to be—the lowest-priced competitor. Unfortunately, the higher-priced competitors are the ones who survive the longest in business and who also make the most profit. (See Chapter 24.)

Pogo Was Right

Several years ago I followed the comic strip "Pogo." Pogo once made the statement, "We have found the enemy and he is us." That particular quote never really left my mind. And I've seen it played out in spades with many of the companies and organizations that I have observed, either as my clients or as the adversaries of my clients.

To put it bluntly, most price-cutting is a self-inflicted wound. And until sales managers or sales reps realize this, they're never going to understand what pricing strategies and tactics are all about in the difficult world of business. Pogo was right: Your competition cannot cut your price. You cut your own price.

It's Illegal for Your Competition to Cut Your Price

When people complain, "My competition is cutting my price—I've got to do something," they fail to understand one basic principle: It is *illegal* for your competition to cut your price. *You* cut your price. No one else cuts your price. Frankly, my advice is that if you find your competition cutting your price, have your competitor jailed.

So you cry loudly, "Obviously *I* set my own price. But that's not what I'm talking about. Of course, my competition can't physically write down the price that *I'm* going to charge. I must do that. I mean that my competition cuts my price by quoting a price that is under the price that I am charging (or quoting to my customer or printing in my catalog or advertisements)."

Of course. But one very serious spin-off is that maybe you are *so sure* that your competition is going to quote a lower price that you cut your price *even before your competition has had a chance to cut his price.* That way you beat your competitor at the turkey's own game. That way you get to it *before* the competitor has an opportunity to louse it up for all you good guys in the industry. That way you get your supply laid in before the hoarders start hoarding things.

I Can Get It Cheaper from Your Competitor

The late G. Marvin Shutt, former Executive Director of the National Sporting Goods Association, had a favorite joke he liked to tell. A customer was talking to the owner of a sporting goods store: "How much are your tennis balls?"

Owner: "They're $3.75 a can."

Customer: "$3.75 a can! Why, that's highway robbery. Why, I can get this same exact tennis ball at your competitor's for $2 a can."

Owner: "Well, gosh, I'm sorry about that. I certainly can't beat a price like that. I guess you'll just have to get your tennis balls from my competitor."

Customer: "I would, but I can't."

Owner: "Why not?"

Customer: "Because your competitor is out of tennis balls right now."

Owner: "Oh—well, come back when I'm out and I'll make you a hell of a deal. Mine are only a buck a can when I'm out."

Obviously, a price is realistic only if they have the merchandise available to provide to the customer upon demand. This underscores the economist's idea that utility is not only in the price of the product (perhaps the lower the better), but also in *having* the product when you want it. If you want to play tennis today but the low-price supplier is out of tennis balls, you're out of luck unless you're willing to pay a higher price. Why should the owner of the sporting goods shop reduce the price on tennis balls just because the competition is charging a lower price on a product they don't even have available to sell?

Yet many people involved in selling products crab and complain about the competitor "cutting the price" because their competition advertises a lower price on merchandise that they have in low supply or a long waiting time on for delivery. These people work avidly to cut their own price to meet the competitor's price, when in fact the competitor's price may not be realistic at all.

Remember, simply saying that you can get something at a lower price elsewhere is *not* a statement of fact. But many sales reps, particularly ones who are not well informed and who would just as soon complain to the sales manager that the price is too high, will capitulate to the suggestion that the customer can get the product at a lower price elsewhere.

One basic fact that just about any truly experienced sales manager understands is that *price is practically always more important in the seller's mind than it is in the buyer's mind.*

Buyers buy for a lot of reasons. Only one of these reasons is price. An experienced seller or sales rep knows that if the price were the only reason that anyone bought anything, only one seller would sell all there is of any given product, service, or commodity.

How Important Is Price in the Purchase Decision?

Many people feel that price is extremely important in the mind of the buyer. Some studies would show that as high as 20–25 percent of our population (both individual consumers and industrial buyers) are essentially price shoppers and buy or make their purchase decision on the basis of the lowest price. But, in truth, very few business operators or consumers actually buy anything on the basis of the lowest price, *irrespective* of other aspects or attributes of the product, service, or commodity they are buying.

Ask yourself this basic question: Are you wearing the cheapest shirt you can buy? Or the cheapest pair of shoes or boots you can buy? Or the cheapest suit you can buy? The answer is, probably not. Now let's go a little bit further. Are you wearing the cheapest watch you could purchase? Are you carrying the cheapest wallet or purse you could buy? Look at your fingers—do you have the cheapest ring on your finger you could buy? You probably did not go out and pay the highest dollar that you could pay. You're probably not wearing million-dollar diamond rings or, for that matter, $400 shirts, $2,000 boots, or $5,000 suits.

In other words, you probably bought most of the goods and services and products you possess, not because of price alone, but because of a complex variety of attributes (including price), all of which boils down to understanding the *competitive edge* under which various products and services are sold.

Of course, you can argue that you *have* made purchase decisions on the basis of price and price alone. Have you ever purchased the cheapest airplane ticket you could buy? Have you ever bought the cheapest gasoline you could find for your automobile? Have you ever bought the cheapest brand of sugar you could buy? Many answer "yes," particularly to the airplane ticket.

But did you *really* buy the *cheapest* airplane ticket you could, or did you buy the cheapest airplane ticket you could get that would take you where you wanted to go? So you wanted to fly from Denver to Honolulu. In all probability you could have bought a cheaper airplane ticket, say from Denver to Salt Lake City, so your purchase decision was based not on price alone, but on the total package: that is, you wanted to get to Honolulu from Denver, not to Salt Lake City. You say you bought the cheapest airplane ticket you could get to take you from Denver to Honolulu? Maybe—or maybe just the cheapest ticket you could get to take you from Denver to Honolulu on the specific day that you could go and on the specific day that you could return. It is literally true that most business travelers pay a far higher price for their airline tickets than do most vacation travelers. The reason is that the business traveler has to go on a specific day: Sunday night or Monday morning, or Thursday afternoon sometime after 2:00 P.M. And they can't lay over the weekend. Or they can't take the 30-day excursion fare, or whatever. So, while they do buy the cheapest ticket they can get, it's *the cheapest ticket they can get that will enable them to do what they must do.* And that is a significant difference. We could find similar discrepancies with the other examples as well, but it all boils down to the fact that people and businesses buy on the basis of price *only as one* of the factors in the purchase decision. There are other competing features about products and services that determine the actual sale.

Understanding Your Competitive Edge

G. Marvin Shutt liked to tell a second story concerning the problem of competitive price cutting. It has to do with one's competitive edge, and it runs as follows:

Customer in sporting goods shop: "How much is that set of golf clubs?"

Owner: "$500 for the set, complete."

Customer: "$500! That's highway robbery. Why, I can get the exact same golf clubs out of this catalog for $450."

Owner: "Well, I certainly can't let you have the golf clubs at that price. I suppose you'll have to buy from your catalog."

Customer: "But you advertise that you will meet or beat any legitimate competitor's price."

Owner: "Of course I'll do that. I advertise that and I'll do it."

Customer: "Well, then you'll have to sell me these clubs at $450 because here's a copy of the catalog, and as you can see it's the exact same set of golf clubs for $450."

Owner: "Oh, well, I'll meet their price. But that's not $450."

Customer: "Well if it's not, what is it? It says right here in the catalog that it's $450."

Owner: "Sure it says $450. But you've got to remember that if you order the golf clubs out of the catalog, you will have to pay freight and insurance, over and above the purchase price, to actually receive the merchandise. Isn't that correct?"

Customer: "Well, yes, I suppose so. But that isn't another $50."

Owner: "Well, how much do you think it is?"

Customer: "Well, it couldn't be more than an additional $25."

Owner: "Okay, if you'll agree that if I charge you a price of $475, and at $475 I'm effectively meeting or beating my competitor's price, I'll sell you the clubs for $475."

Customer: "Okay, I'll agree. That sounds like you're effectively meeting or beating their price."

Owner: "Okay, give me your credit card." (Owner processes credit card voucher and customer signs. Owner returns credit card to the customer and turns around and walks off.)

Customer: "Hey, where you going? Give me my golf clubs."

Owner: "Nope, you've got to wait one week for delivery, just like out of the catalog. However, if you'd like to play golf with these clubs today, I can let you have them now for an extra $25."

This story underscores again the case of having the right product at the right place at the right time. But more than underscoring the fact that time utility is important, it underscores the fact that ability to deliver the product is also significant. Most all businesses, whether they are retailers or service industries, manufacturers or wholesalers, compete on five different bases. That comprises your competitive edge.

Price is one we've already discussed. All products are sold on the basis of their competitive edge in the marketplace. Another is the quality of the merchandise, product, or service which is being sold. A third element is the service provided with those products, goods, and services. Still another is the ability of the seller to deliver the product that is desired, when it is desired, and where it is desired, and in the form and shape and size in which it is desired. Finally, products are also sold on the basis of salesmanship or the advertising and promotion that goes into alerting the customer that the product is available for purchase.

Price Is a Purchase Decision

If price were the only reason that anybody bought anything, only one supplier would supply all of that commodity to the marketplace. That supplier would be the one who sold at the lowest price. But, as indicated by personal purchases such as shirts and shoes, suits and rings, typically you make the purchase decisions on other factors, which include the quality of the product, the style, the convenience, the service, etc.

Quality of the Product

Sometimes we buy things on the basis of the quality of the product, not on the basis of price. Sometimes we want the best. Sometimes we want something that will last. Sometimes we want something that has a finer texture or a finer flavor or a more pleasing smell or touch.

The value of quality can hardly be argued when you compare a shoddy product with a truly quality product. Most everyone has seen an original oil painting, and most everyone has seen a printed copy of a painting. In essence, they are the same and, supposedly, serve the same purpose: to provide decor for a wall or room. But which is better? Obviously, the original has more depth of color and is more pleasing to the eye. In short, it has a *quality* that the reproduction cannot attain. But, the price is certainly a great deal higher than the copy.

Or consider a designer suit versus one off the rack at your local discount store. Certainly the discount variety will be much less expensive, and both will allow you to go out in public without getting arrested for obscenity. But the discount suit may fall apart the first time it is cleaned—or before—and probably won't feel or look as nice—and you won't feel as elegantly dressed as you would with the more expensive item.

So the quality of a product has a lot to do with whether or not it is bought. But service is also important.

Service to the Customer

Many products are bought on the basis of the service provided by the seller. Does the seller, for example, extend credit to the buyer? Many people who argue that they always buy on the lowest price often go to a seller who's not the lowest priced, but who gives them credit or permits them to use a credit card. Many industrial buyers who argue that they only buy on the basis of the lowest price will go and place an order from a supplier who delivers overnight (since the buyer is going to have to shut down his production line because of lack of parts if that overnight service isn't provided).

Manufacturers of heavy machinery and equipment used in construction often provide this service to their clients. If your bulldozer or your backhoe is broken and so your people will be out of work and you'll miss a contract completion schedule, isn't it worth a little something to have a supplier who will air freight a five-ton engine to your job site, rather than have one who will sell it to you at the lowest price but ship it by boat? Of course service counts. But service, like quality, costs. Genuine leather invariably costs more than cheap vinyl. Air freighting parts invariably costs more than sending it by boat. But often the quality and service is more important than the price, because the price pales in comparison to other costs incurred if the product disintegrates in use and/or if machinery and equipment can't be used.

Ability to Deliver

Many customers overlook the value of a supplier who has a product that is needed when it is needed. The stories about the tennis balls and golf clubs above pretty well attest to that. But probably more significant is the question of whether or not the supplier will deliver.

There are very few manufacturers whose purchasing agents buy on price alone. Most any experienced purchasing agent will tell you that when they buy they try to assume that they are getting the quality they need, the service that is expected, *and* that the parts or material which they are buying will be delivered when promised. One of my clients reports that his toughest "price buyer" tells him that if he is even three days late on delivery, the job goes back out for competitive bids. Is that customer more concerned about price or delivery?

Ability to deliver ties in with service. Will the parts be delivered at all? It is not unusual for low-price bidders, who are financially strapped for cash, to bid or quote a price on a product that they aren't even sure they can manufacture—or, if they do, they're not going to be able to hold the kinds of quality tolerances required for the product. Thus, they simply can't deliver the product they advertised. So what are you going to do if they don't deliver? Sue them? They're probably already financially strapped—perhaps bankrupt—but simply haven't gotten around to filing the papers yet. So what can you gain because you placed an order that won't be delivered? Your business fails because your assembly line is shut down, and you in turn can't make your deliveries.

Sales Capability

The fifth reason that most products and services are bought is sales capability, advertising, and promotion talent. The fact is that many of your sales representatives will tell you that they can sell—and it will be true if the product is selling—but these same reps will tell you that something is wrong with the product (such as the price is too high) if they are not selling the product. (As discussed in Chapter 19, sales reps always want to take credit for selling things when they are sold, but don't want to take any credit for failing to sell when the product doesn't move.)

Let's face it, there *is* something to sales capability. Some people can sell things and some people can't. Furthermore, there *is* some value to a decent advertisement or promotional piece compared to a schlocky operation. If indeed you are really convinced that you have crackerjack sales personnel and one of the finest advertising agents in the country and you have positioned your product squarely and visibly in the minds of the buyers, then why does your sales rep have to sell at a lower price? It costs money to advertise. It costs money to keep sales reps on the road. It costs money to demonstrate products and services. It costs money to provide samples. So if your sales representation techniques are so good, how come your price has to be low?

Who Really Cuts Your Price?

This discussion of competitive edge pretty well determines the fact that, not only is it true from a legalistic stance that your competition is not cutting your price, it is also true that you deliberately, with malice aforethought, are the price-cutter and that you cut your own price. This usually occurs because of lack of understanding of your competitive edge. Commodities, products, and services are sold basically on five counts—quality, service, ability to deliver, advertising, and price—but they are *not* sold on the basis of price alone. Price is only *one* feature of the product. If your competition keeps "cutting your price," remember the immortal words of Pogo: "We have found the enemy and he is us."

21

We Make It Up in Volume

The old joke about "We sell below cost, but we make it up in volume" is older than the hills and describes a situation no one could possibly believe. Obviously, it is *not possible* to sell below cost and hope to make it up in volume, no matter how high the volume gets.

So no one can really believe that "We make it up in volume." Management is just common sense—yet the joke seems to be on us. While everybody would agree it's impossible to make it up in volume, and everybody knows the error of that logic, *we still seem to run our businesses predicated upon the belief that we can somehow make it up in volume!*

The Folly of Price Cutting

Any knowledgeable business executive should be aware of the fact that you must cover your costs and then some if you're going to operate profitably. But very few actually understand how much *additional* volume must be generated to make up for a very modest "competitive" price reduction.

For example, on the very day I began writing this chapter, I conducted a seminar entitled "Pricing by Objectives for Manufacturers." I asked the 28 executives attending the seminar how much volume they would need to make up for a 10-percent price cut, if they averaged a maintained gross profit margin of 40 percent. Estimates ranged from a 20-percent to an 80-percent increase.

On a separate note pad you might indicate how much volume increase *you* think would be necessary to make up a 10 percent price cut if you have been working on a maintained gross profit margin of 40 percent. (Incidentally, this same volume is necessary if you are *slow, timid* or *reluctant* about *raising* your prices and, by default because of inflation, take a de facto 10 percent price cut.)

I then asked them how much volume they could afford to lose and still make as much money, if they *raised* their prices by 10 percent—again assuming that they operated on a maintained gross profit margin of 40 percent.

Again, write on the note pad how much physical sales loss could be realized and still make just as much money as a result of the 10 percent price hike.

The Swings in Volume Necessary to Make Up for Being Underpriced or Overpriced

If your numbers are fairly typical of a manufacturing company, and you maintain a gross profit margin of 40 percent, you will have to increase your physical sales volume by 67 percent to make up for a 10-percent cut in price. Yet, if you increase your price by 10 percent, at the same gross profit margin, you can lose almost 30 percent of your sales (actual calculation is 29 percent) and still make just as much money.

If your gross profit margin is lower than the 40-percent example (and most manufacturers run between 30 and 35 percent) the swing is *even wider.* For a 10-percent underprice position with a gross margin of 35 percent, you actually have to *double* your volume to make up for your too-low price; while if your price is 10 percent higher, you can lose 34 percent of your physical volume and still make just as much money.

But How Can That Be So?

You may wonder, "But how can that be so? After all, you're talking about virtually doubling my volume if I'm only 10 percent underpriced, while you're telling me that I can lose nearly a third of my business if I'm 10 percent overpriced and still make just as much money. That's impossible. Prove it!"

Check out what happens to your margins when you change prices. First, take a look at a typical profit and loss statement. Assume a profit-and-loss statement in which the manufacturer is doing the following. (Incidentally, the numbers work the same for the retailer, but the ratios will be a little different. Most well-run retailer stores will have a 40–45-percent gross profit margin.)

Sales	$1,000,000	100%
Cost of goods sold	600,000	60%
Gross margin	$ 400,000	40%
GS&A expenses:		
Fixed GS&A expenses	250,000	25%
Variable GS&A expenses	150,000	15%
Profit	0	

As illustrated, this company is breaking even. It is making no money, which is a good point to calculate if we change prices, because when we change prices, what we change is the gross margin. So let's see how a price change (in the following example a price cut) changes the gross margin. And then we'll see how and why, *at these new margins*, our price volume has to increase so dramatically to be able to come back to our breakeven point.

What Happens If We Cut Our Price by 10 Percent?

Take the foregoing profit-and-loss statment and assume that the price is cut by 10 percent. For the moment, assume that the sales volume does not change. We can observe the effect of a price cut on the various margins in relationship to sales volume. In that situation our profit-and-loss statement would look like this:

Sales	$900,000	100%
Cost of goods sold	600,000	66.7%
Gross margin	$300,000	33.3%
GS&A expenses:		
Fixed GS&A expenses	250,000	28%
Variable GS&A expenses	150,000	16.7%
Profit	(100,000)	

So, when we reduce our selling price by 10 percent, our cost of goods sold increases from 60 percent of sales to 67 percent of the selling price, and our gross margin falls from $400,000 to $300,000. Our gross margin, therefore, becomes only 33 percent of our selling price, because our selling price now is $100,000 lower in total revenues. This is because we lowered our price by 10 percent on the million dollars in sales, and because we are assuming, *for the moment*, that our sales volume does not change. Thus, we would lose the full $100,000 because of the loss in revenues generated due to the cut in price (the full $100,000 will pass through to the bottom line as an operating loss).

But When You Cut Price
You Increase Volume

When you cut your price, you are supposed to increase your sales volume.* If it is true that the volume will increase as a result of our price cut, then the only thing we need to calculate is *how much* volume increase must be *at our new margins* to make up for the price cut. The next profit-and-loss statement will show that our volume in sales must increase to $1,500,000 (a 50-percent increase in sales).

To calculate what our sales volume must be, look at the new percentages and ratios. Created because of the lower price, they show that our costs of goods sold are approximately 67 percent on sales, our gross profit margin is 33 percent on sales, and our variable expenses are 16.7 percent on sales (now that we're selling our product at a price which is 90 cents on the dollar that our product used to fetch). These new ratios have been created because our selling price has been reduced to 90 cents on the dollar, but our cost of goods sold does not change (it will cost the same amount to produce the same volume— remember, we are selling the same volume). Therefore, our

---

* Supposedly our volume will increase. But there are notable cases where, when the price is cut, the volume declines. This is a result of the phenomenon where the customer begins to feel that the product is probably shoddy, because "if anything is that cheap, it can't be worth very much." This is unusual, but can and does occur.

gross margin, being the difference between the cost of goods sold and the selling price, becomes a new percentage of our selling price.

Our variable expenses in GS&A also become a new percentage of our selling price because our selling price has been reduced. In fact, the only costs that remain constant are our fixed costs, which by definition do not change. They are $250,000. Plugging in those relationships, we can see the givens in the following profit-and-loss statement. Therefore, all we need to do is calculate which dollar figures need to be filled in at those percentages or ratios to permit us to come back to a breakeven volume of sales. If there is a number that serves to fill in as the sales volume and that can be multiplied by the cost-of-goods-sold percent on sales (67 percent) and the gross margin percent on sales (33 percent) and the variable expense percent (16.7 percent) and come out to breakeven, then we will have calculated how much volume change is necessary to make up for a price cut.

As stated above, the number that can be put in for the sales figure which will calculate out at all the relevant percentages and come out at a breakeven volume is $1,500,000.

Sales	$1,500,000	100%
Cost of goods sold	1,000,000	66.7%
Gross margin	500,000	33.3%
GS&A expenses:		
Fixed GS&A expenses	$ 250,000	
Variable GS&A expenses	250,000	16.7%
Profit	0	

Thus, we see that once the price is cut, the volume required to break even changes rather dramatically, because of the relationship of the selling price to all the other operational costs that do not go down simply because the price goes down.

But Don't the Costs of Goods Sold
Go Down as Volume Increases?

Anyone who analyzes the foregoing is probably going to say "Yeah, but..." And what they mean by that is, "Yeah, but isn't it true that your cost of goods sold will go down as your volume increases? It's not realistic to assume that your cost of goods sold will remain a constant percentage of sales when you are significantly increasing your volume."

It is true that *probably* your cost of goods sold will go down as your volume increases—*for a while!* But then they'll start going back up. Remember, we're increasing physical sales volume by 67 percent (that can be calculated by the cost-of-goods-sold figure). That is, at the old volume, cost-of-goods sold was $600,000. At the new sales volume, cost of goods sold is $1,000,000. Those are *costs-of-production* dollars and therefore show our *physical* volume of production. This shows a 67-percent increase in the physical volume of sales that must be realized to have the profit-and-loss statement come back to a breakeven volume.

Some people erroneously believe that sales volume will only have to increase by 50 percent to make up for the 10-percent price cut (claiming that sales increased from $1,000,000 to $1,500,000). That is true, and it is only a 50-percent increase. But remember, the $1,500,000 sales volume is in 90-cent dollars. That is, that dollar sales volume is generated from a sales price of the product that is now only 90 cents on the dollar. Thus, the only way to accurately calculate what the *physical sales volume* increase must be to make up for the price cut is to calculate the change from the *old* cost of goods sold to the *new* cost of goods sold—and that shows a 67-percent increase.

Something else must be understood. Seldom does a manufacturer who's running along at a production-efficient volume go below 50 percent of potential volume. Thus, if we have to increase our physical sales volume by 67 percent, and we are at 50 percent of our capacity, we suddenly must kick our production volume from 50 percent of capacity up to 83 percent of capacity. And any production genius will tell you that, while it is true that as our production volume increases, our production costs go *down* to a point, it is also true that, as our production volume begins to approach our capacity, our production costs start *going back up.* This is a phenomenon true in most industries and explored in greater detail in Chapter 23. Suffice it to say here that it is valid to assume that the cost-of-goods sold as a percentage of sales will *not* go down as a percentage of sales, particularly when someone has cut their price in order to increase sales volume or meet a competitor's price. This is notwithstanding the fact that, in the short run, unit production costs *may* go down as manufacturing volume goes up, if there is a lot of excess capacity. It simply is *not* true when you begin to approach your capacity. And when we're talking about a 67-percent increase in physical production volume, most companies are going to approach that physical barrier. Many exceed it. Just think about what would happen if you were operating at 60 percent of your capacity. A 67-percent increase of 60 percent of your capacity calculates out to exactly 100 percent of your capacity—a virtual impossibility. So you know something will blow if you need the kind of volume increase generated as a result of an idiotic 10-percent reduction in price or as a result of being slow at raising prices. And, remember, you still haven't made a penny extra—you've just stayed even and worked harder. Yet people still feel they can "make it up in volume."

What Happens When You Raise Your Price?

It is extremely difficult, if not impossible, to get enough physical volume increase in sales to make up for a price cut with the finite markets and resources available to most manufacturing operations—either to generate the sales volume or to manufacture the required product. But what many otherwise astute business people do not realize is that, contrariwise, as significant an amount of volume can be *lost* if prices are too high because of, again, what happens to the margins.

This is how it works. Consider again the basic breakeven model developed earlier.

Sales	$1,000,000	100%
Cost of goods sold	600,000	60%
Gross margin	$ 400,000	40%
GS&A expenses:		
Fixed GS&A expenses	250,000	25%
Variable GS&A expenses	150,000	15%
Profit	0	

Now assume that you raise your selling price by 10 percent and, again for the moment, assume that your sales volume does not change. What happens to your gross margin as a result of our price increases? It looks like this:

Sales	$1,100,000	100%
Cost of goods sold	600,000	54.5%
Gross margin	500,000	45.4%
GS&A expenses:		
Fixed GS&A expenses	250,000	22.7%
Variable GS&A expenses	150,000	13.6%
Profit	$ 100,000	9%

Thus, as a result of raising your price by 10 percent and realizing the same exact sales volume, your net profit will increase from 0 to $100,000. The price increase passes clear through to the bottom line.

But again, in the real world we assume that sales volume will probably decline as a result of price increases. The question is, again at the new margins, how low can that dollar sales volume figure sink and still calculate out to a breakeven point?

Sales	$785,714	100%
Cost of goods sold	428,571	54.5%
Gross margin	357,143	45.4%
GS&A expenses		
Fixed GS&A expenses	250,000	
Variable GS&A expenses	107,143	13.6%
Profit	0	

At the new ratios, you will break even at $785,714 in sales volume. More specifically, however, while you can only lose 21 percent of your dollar *sales* volume if you raise your price (falling from a breakeven $1 million in sales to a new breakeven of $785,714), your physical volume of sales can decline 29 percent (down from the original breakeven cost-of-goods-sold physical sales volume of $600,000 to the new one of $428,571).

Therefore, at a price increase of 10 percent, you can probably lose 29 percent of your physical sales volume and *still make as much money.* In contrast, if your price is 10 percent too low, you will have to increase your physical sales volume by 67 percent to make up for the too-low price.

Consider one other thing. While mathematically it is true that you can lose 29 percent of your volume, in actuality you can probably lose even more physical sales volume and still make the same amount of money, or at least break even! The reason is because, while the numbers show that you can lose 29 percent of the physical sales volume, practically always when you lose a customer because of price, *you are losing the most expensive customer to whom you are selling!*

"Come on," you say, "what are you talking about—expensive customer?" The customer who is the most price-sensitive inevitably is the one who costs you the most to sell to; that is, they take the longest time to sell, so your selling expenses go up. Furthermore, they are the ones who are most apt to find fault with your product and return it, raise hell because it isn't any good, require you to come out and replace it/repair it/exchange it (meanwhile you're bearing all the costs of freight, telephone calls, etc.), and refuse to pay until you "make it right." And while they're refusing to pay you, the interest costs run up on the money you've got tied up in inventory you produced and sold to them. The same holds true for the labor costs incorporated in the product you sold and other associated costs attributed to the product you manufactured and shipped to them. Then, practically always, the one to whom the price is the most dear is the one who doesn't have anyone in the office to sign the check, has the check "in the mail" but it apparently got lost, and/or who lost your invoice after you got the product problems straightened out.

If you throw all those costs in, it's highly likely that your most expensive GS&A fixed-and-variable costs are expended on those customers to whom the price makes the most difference. You seldom find the customer of a less price-conscious nature who is slow paying, argumentative, or deliberately tries to drag out the day of reconciliation of accounts.

Sit Back and Think About Your Business

One more point must be made about the fact that if you raise your price, you can lose some volume and perhaps make some more money.

While I argued that you must increase your physical sales volume by 67 percent as a result of a 10-percent price cut, I glossed over the fact that this kind of physical volume increase makes things a little hectic around the shop. Nobody has time to do anything. Things get neglected. Everybody's running flat out. None of the little things that *need* to be done ever seem *to get done.*

On the contrary, if you raise your price you may get a slowdown (being able to afford it) and have time to sit back and *think* about your business. Perhaps you can now take the time to prop your feet on the table and plan where you're going, how you're going to get there, and most importantly, how you're going to get there *profitably.*

Furthermore, you might be able to do a little maintenance. And you might even be able to slow down production to a *more efficient level!* For example, if you've been running at 90 percent of your capacity and you realize a 30 percent physical volume of sales loss, you're now running at about 63 percent of capacity. You may actually slide back down to a more efficient productivity schedule, in which case your cost of goods sold, relative to your selling price, will actually go down. (This is what you expected to happen when you increased your sales volume as a result of a price cut.) Most manufacturers have a finite limit to their productive capacity, and most try to run at higher levels of productivity. It is not unusual to discover that people can not only slow down the hectic pace of business, they can actually think about what's going on, and realize economies of scale in production cost as a result.

If You're Going to Fail in Business Because of a Pricing Error, Always Fail Because You Overprice

When I was growing up, I had an old Ford. As luck would have it, I needed a fuel pump for it. So I went into the local auto parts shop to buy one.

When the dealer produced the fuel pump, I asked how much it was. He quoted what I thought was an extraordinarily high price, so I gave him a lecture about how he was going to go out of business if he didn't learn the meaning of "fair" price (fair to me, of course, not to him).

This dealer told me, "Sonny, my daddy always told me, if you're going to fail in business, you should fail because you're overpricing, not because you're underpricing."

My reply was, "What do you mean by that?" He said, "Look at it this way. If I fail in my business because I'm underpricing and I work it just right, the day I die will be the day the sheriff locks up my front door. But if I fail because I've been overpricing, all I need to do is sit back, light up a cigar, and take it easy. The net effect is the same. It just doesn't take as much work to fail for overpricing as it does for underpricing."

I never forgot that bit of philosophy. It was a lesson well learned. And, like many from the back woods areas of America, the man was wise beyond his apparent means. And there certainly is truth to what he said. If you are going to fail because you are underpricing, you are going to work like hell to be an underpricing fool. If the net effect is, nevertheless, failure in business, you should remember that it doesn't take near the work, or effort, or the feverish activity to fail when you are overpricing.

So How Can I Tell If My Price Is Too High or Too Low?

Because of the extraordinarily wide swings in volume increases necessary to underprice and the amount of volume you may lose if you overprice, it is necessary to include some of the indicators of both overpricing and underpricing.

Indicators of Overpricing

What are the major indicators that might signal the overpricing of your products or services in your business? They include the following:
1. Your competitor's prices are lower than yours.
2. Your gross profit percentage is growing—but your sales are not.
3. You receive many customer complaints (or inquiries) about what is or is not included in your price.

4. Your dollar sales volume is declining.
5. Your competition's percent or share of the market is increasing.
6. Your salespeople are receiving many price complaints. (But watch for your own salespeople causing or inviting the complaints or encouraging customers to complain.)
7. Whenever there is a request for an adjustment because of a faulty or defective product or service, the complaint is actually disguised as a price complaint, rather than a true complaint about the quality of the product.
8. Your wholesale buyer seriously asks, "Is that the retail price?"
9. Your manufacturer's rep says, "If I take less commission, can I sell it at a lower price?"

To a large degree, these overpricing factors apply to manufacturers, but they also apply to wholesalers and retailers, as well as people in the construction and service industries. Underpricing seems more serious.

Indicators of Underpricing

1. Your gross profit percentage is getting smaller on the same or rising sales volume.
2. Your net profit margin is getting smaller on the same or rising sales volume.
3. Your prices are below your competitors.
4. There's a lot of talk by your customers about "how good" or "how much better run" your company is than your competitors.
5. There is a general absence of any complaints about price.
6. Prices have not been changed over a long period of time during known inflationary pressures.
7. Customers buy without haggling over price or asking about what is or is not included in the price—or don't even bother to ask the price.
8. You're getting many new customers for no apparent reason or effort on your part.
9. There is a sudden upsurge in business volume, particularly from *new* customers.

10. Your customers insist that, if there is faulty or defective product, you've got to make the product work or replace it, rather than refund their money.
11. Your labor and materials costs have increased without increases in your prices.
12. Someone who is a known price buyer starts buying from you.
13. You have a big backlog of demand, particularly if your backlog of demand exceeds the average for those in your industry or with whom you compete.
14. Your customers buy more than they need—and you know it.
15. Your bad debt collection procedures are increasing in activity.
16. You are getting your competitor's credit cutoff business.
17. You know your customer's gross margin, it is getting bigger, and your product represents a significant portion of your customer's cost-of-goods sold.
18. Your salespeople *stop* complaining about your price being too high.
19. Your "request for quotations" increases dramatically, especially for no particular reason.
20. Your "kill rate" or success rate or percentage on winning "jobs bid" begins to increase.
21. Your representative says, "Okay, if I sell at a higher price, can I keep one-half of the overage?"
22. Your gut feeling just tells you that the product will probably carry a higher price in the marketplace.
23. Your customer's buyer would like to come to work for you.
24. Your competitor's representatives start complaining to *your* customers about you and how you do business.
25. A new potential distributor for your products is already bootlegging your products.
26. Your competition bows out and can't compete with you anymore because they went broke.
27. Your customers quit buying from you but then come back to you.
28. Your manufacturer's representative (a) grabs the lunch check, (b) pays in cash, (c) does not need a receipt.

29. A competitor of yours wants to buy from you *and* (a)
    says he can't make his shipping schedule *and* (b) wants
    you to private label (especially if producing the product
    requires tooling on your part).
30. Your customer comes to your office.
31. Your customer asks, "Is this price list still in effect?"
As can be seen from the foregoing list, some of these are slanted
toward the manufacturer's indicators of underpricing. However, most of them can again be translated into similar indicators for the retailer, wholesaler, construction industry or service industry business.

Guess We Can't Make It Up in Volume

Everybody knows that you can't make it up in volume, but
not everybody knows just *how true that is*. Most people feel
that if you lower your price *a little*, because of increased production efficiencies and greater amounts of product demanded
you can make up for that price cut with volume increases. And
while mathematically it is possible to make up in volume for
those price cuts, very few people actually realize how significant those swings have to be.

One last note should probably be made about those volume
changes. Assumptions used here concerned a gross profit
margin of 40 percent. For any business whose gross profit
margin is less (meaning 35, 30, 25, 20, etc.), the lower the gross
margin, *the wider the swings must be*. That is, at a gross profit
margin of 35 percent, you must double your volume if your
price is 10 percent lower, and yet you could lose roughly one-
third of your volume if your price is 10 percent higher. At a
25-percent gross profit margin, if you are 10 percent lower, your
physical sales volume increase must be 300 percent, and you
can lose nearly 50 percent of your business and still make up
for having a 10-percent higher price.

So everybody knows the answer to the "truth" of this
chapter. You can't make it up in volume. You knew that. What
you didn't know, perhaps, was how close you couldn't come.

22

The Demand Curve Slopes Downward and to the Right

If you ever took Econ 101 at any U.S. college or university, you probably learned that "The demand curve slopes downward and to the right."

The truth behind this idea is based on the fact that, when explaining the demand for a product being sold, it is customary to plot price on a vertical axis and quantity sold on the horizontal axis. Because at a high price very few items are sold, and at a low price many are sold, a demand curve slopes downward and to the right.

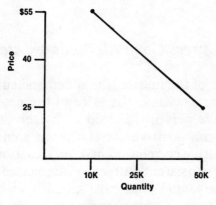

FIGURE 22-1

As the accompanying graph shows, at a selling price of $55 for a pair of running shoes, a manufacturer might be able to sell 10,000 pairs. However, if the same running shoes were offered at a lower price, say $40, the manufacturer might sell 25,000 pairs of shoes. But if the selling price were *really* lowered to a bargain level, say $25 per pair, maybe the manufacturer would sell 50,000 pairs.

What? The Demand Curve Doesn't Slope Downward and to the Right?

Any astute economics professor knows full well that the standard demand curve, like Figure 22-1, is simply one way to demonstrate general economic events. When given the pleasure of teaching Econ 101, that instructor is going to teach the simplest things in the simplest way possible—and the standard demand curve is part of that simplicity. Furthermore, most students aren't interested in learning advanced micro-economic (or macro-economic) theory and therefore don't want to know about all the other variations that the demand curve (or a cost curve or a marginal utility curve or a marginal revenue curve) might take.

This "truth" is taught simply as a starting point. Unfortunately, not very many students follow economics past the starting point and, because they end their economics education with the Econ 101 final exam, they never learn anything more about economics. They believe that what they have learned is true and that's it.

Demand Curves Go in All Kinds of Directions

The *real* truth of the matter is that demand curves go in all kinds of directions, because the price of the product and the quantity sold have very little to do with each other in some cases, interact on a positive correlation in some situations, interact on a negative correlation in other situations, and occasionally have no consistent pattern of interaction whatsoever.

Most sales personnel (and most managers who have anything to do with the sale of the product or service) believe that the demand for their product will be enhanced if their price is lowered, and the demand for their product will diminish if their price is raised or if their price is too high.

As Chapter 21 showed, there is every reason in the world to sell a product at a high price and not much justification to sell a product at a lower price. But still the belief remains: "We can make it up in volume. This is particularly true if we lower the price, because we can sell ever so much more. After all, as I learned in Econ class..."

Even in Econ 101 the Demand Curve Didn't Always Slope Downward and to the Right

Your Econ instructor probably did point out that a demand curve doesn't necessarily slope downward and to the right, or more accurately, "While it usually does, the angle of the slope may vary quite a lot." The professor probably explained about the shifting steepness of the grade of the demand curve as being couched in terms of price elasticity and price inelasticity.*

Price elasticity essentially means that if the *demand* for a product changes very greatly in response to a *very small change* in price, there is *high price elasticity*; whereas if the demand changes very *little*, even for an *extremely high change* in price, the demand for the product is very price inelastic. The two classic examples used to illustrate this principle concern salt and a loss leader in the grocery store.

Salt Isn't Elastic

Each household tends to consume a certain amount of table salt in any given year—no more, no less. Therefore, the typical household will buy only so much table salt in a year's time, and this, spread over all households in the United States, means that only so much table salt will be sold each year. In other words, we need a certain quantity of salt, but we only need so much, and the quantity isn't large. Therefore, the demand curve for table salt is usually illustrated as follows:

---

* Don't panic. You don't have to understand these terms. There aren't any more tests in this book.

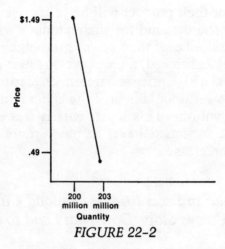

FIGURE 22-2

The graph above shows table salt is sold at $1.49 per pound. There may be 200 million pounds of table salt sold in a year's time. However, if table salt is reduced to 49 cents per pound, there may be 203 million pounds sold in a year's time. As long as the price remains "ballpark reasonable," there probably won't be any more or any less table salt sold in any appreciable degree. Now admittedly, if table salt were reduced to 3 cents per pound, people might buy table salt and use it to salt their driveways and sidewalks during snow season. But generally speaking, only so much table will be sold, irrespective of fairly broad changes in the price.

Loss Leaders Are Elastic

It is also suggested that a demand curve, while sloping downward and to the right, sometimes has a horizontal surface with very little slant to it (but the slant is downward and to the right). The example used for that kind of a demand curve is invariably a loss leader at the grocery store. Everyone "knows" the price something normally sells at, but occasionally someone offers a deal on that price to stimulate a high volume of sale of that product in that store.

Consider, for example, a special price on ground beef at the supermarket. If hamburger is selling for $2 a pound, the supermarket will sell so much (say, 400 pounds per day). However, if a special price is offered on that hamburger (say, $1.50 a pound), then that supermarket might increase the demand for the hamburger twenty-fold.

Plotting the demand for the loss-leader hamburger on the accompanying graph shows the demand curve to be relatively flat, but it also slopes downward and to the right because the volume of sales was increased greatly for a very small change in price.

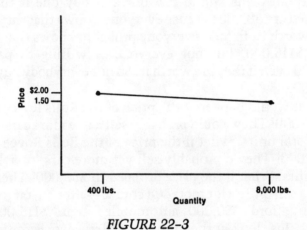

FIGURE 22-3

The foregoing example is probably about as far as you got in Econ 101 and, if that was the last course you took, you probably didn't learn a lot about kinky demand curves (doesn't have anything to do with sex habits necessarily) and other exotic fare to be found in advanced courses in economics.

Kinky Demand Curves

Kinky demand curves do exist, and they have a whale of a lot to do with the way products are really sold—and the kinds of pricing strategies and marketing decisions sales personnel should understand when it comes to selling a product effectively in the marketplace.

Demand curves become kinky because they get kinks in them. They get kinks in them because the angle or direction of the demand curve begins to shift somewhat. For example, have you ever considered what the demand curve for a Rolls Royce must look like? It must slope downward and to the right, doesn't it? They all do.

The answer is, probably not so. Now, the Rolls Royce is a fine automobile. And about 3,500 of them are sold per year. The significant bulk is sold in the U.S. market at an average price of perhaps $115,000 per unit.

Now what if the people who sell Rolls Royce automobiles lowered their price? Would they sell more? Of course— probably all of us would run out and buy one if they were marketed at $58,000 because everyone knows that they are certainly worth it. In fact, everyone probably knows that they are worth $115,000, but not everyone is willing to part with $115,000 even if they *are* worth it. So not everybody buys one at $115,000.

What would happen if the price of the Rolls Royce dropped to $100,000? They would probably sell a few more cars—maybe 4,000 total units. What if the price of the Rolls Royce dropped to $75,000? They'd probably sell yet more cars—maybe 5,000 total units. What if the price dropped to $50,000? Then they'd begin to sell quite a lot more? Of course—after all, far more people can afford $50,000 automobiles than $115,000 automobiles. Just look at the number of Mercedes, Ferraris, Excaliburs, Alfa Romeos, Zimmers, Clenets, Valientes, etc., that are sold at that price.

But this is all *wrong!* If Rolls Royce reduced their price to $50,000, it may be true that many more people could afford to buy one. But the problem is that while many people who would otherwise buy a Mercedes, Ferrari, or Alfa might switch to buying Rolls Royces, it is also likely that many of the people who have been buying Rolls Royces at $115,000 would no longer buy them because "everybody and their dog is buying one."

In fact, it could well be that if Rolls Royce reduced their price to $50,000, or perhaps lower, they would actually end up selling fewer cars! It could be that they would drive off the upper-class market to whom they cater because they are encouraging the lower class riffraff market to purchase their products. And if the price of a Rolls Royce were dropped to the $20,000–$25,000 range, they could lose not only sales to the upper-crust typical Rolls Royce buyer, but also some people would begin to become suspicious of the quality of the Rolls

Royce car and not buy it *even though they could afford it* because, after all, anything *that* cheap probably isn't any good.

The demand curve for a Rolls Royce probably has a kink in it. While it starts off sloping downward and to the right, it may then continue to slope downward, but to the left! The accompanying graph represents a kinky demand curve that the producers of Rolls Royce might consider in manufacturing and selling their product. And if they see their demand curve looking like this, they may never lower their price to increase volume.

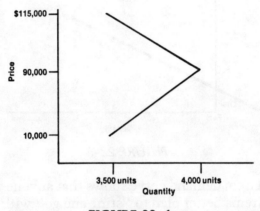

FIGURE 22–4

Is the kinky demand curve for the Rolls Royce realistic? Probably so. But the Rolls Royce is the exception, not the everyday, run-of-the-mill product on the market. But other kinky demand curves exist, and they have a lot to do with the way your product is sold and the "common sense" of management.

The kinky demand curve for the Rolls Royce argues that their prices should remain high. But what about the almost similar looking kinky demand curve that exists for fad items?

Fad Item Demand Curves

Perhaps you remember the "mood ring" or the hula hoop and, of course, there's always last year's hottest fashion item that you wouldn't be caught dead in this year.

If you are marketing and selling fad items, you had better know what kind of a kinky demand curve exists for fad items. The accompanying demand curve shows that at a high price a few things are sold; if you lower the price, a few more are sold. If you lower the price again, no more are sold because the fad has dried up. In fact, if you lower the price to zero, you may not even be able to give them away.

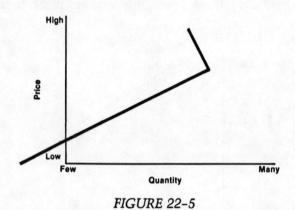

FIGURE 22-5

The fad item demand curve shows that anyone who's going to sell fad items better plan to "sting and go" with their price. Don't count on the fact that the demand curve slopes downward and to the right. Rely on the fact that the demand curve probably drops very precipitously, so you may as well charge a high price to skim the market and not worry about the future.

But Sometimes Fads Hit

Not all fad items end up as fads. Sometimes fads hit and stay in the marketplace. In fact, sometimes fads hit so well that they become timeless necessities. The kinky demand curve for this type of product looks something like the accompanying graph.

It shows that at a certain relatively high price a fad item is introduced to the market. That fad might be something like a food processor. Then, when one lowers the price slightly, a few

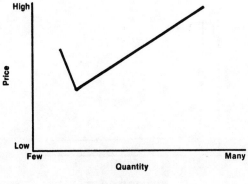

FIGURE 22-6

more units are sold. Then, when one lowers the price again, still more units are sold. But by this time the fad is becoming more than a fad. It is being viewed as a *necessity!* Then the supplier of the fad item decides that the fad is going to stick, so the thing to do is to *raise* the price to extract additional revenues if at all possible. So they raise the price of the item. And yet more units are sold because the fad *is* going to stick and has caught on. Then they begin to raise the price even more to try to enhance profitability of their firm. Therefore we get a demand curve that looks like Figure 22-6.

Sliding Down the Demand Curve

The last demand curve we will consider shows that the demand curve starts at a very high price and that a very small volume is sold. If the price is lowered ever so slightly, a few more are sold. If the price is lowered slightly more, a few *more* are sold—until some point is reached where the rate of sale increases fairly dramatically and the demand curve gets almost horizontally flat (not unlike that in the loss-leader situation of Figure 22-3).

As Figure 22-7 demonstrates, that kind of demand curve indicates that a product may start out at a very high price and be sold in ever-so-slightly increasing quantities as the price is dropped; but at some point with a not very great price drop, suddenly the volume sold is virtually unbelievable.

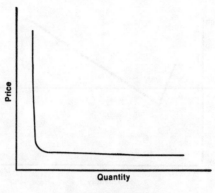

Price

Quantity

FIGURE 22-7

The History of the Ballpoint Pen

One good example of the kind of product that would track very closely to the demand curve in Figure 22-7 is that of the ordinary ballpoint pen.

When ballpoint pens were first introduced on the market, they cost in the neighborhood of $25. These pens were not even as good as the cheapest one you've got lying around your house that probably has advertising information on it and didn't cost you a penny—and the total cost to the advertiser was probably less than 10 cents.

This isn't such an unusual example, either. Many products have demand curves similar to that of the ballpoint pen. You may have another in your pocket or purse: the pocket calculator.

As recently as 1970 it was possible for very astute purchasing agents in large organizations to buy digital calculators for as much as $3,500 and they wouldn't do what your basic $15 pocket calculator will do today. The same is true of color television sets, or even the original black-and-white television set, or, for that matter, practically anything associated in the electronic industry.

All of this points out that in the real world it is definitely *not* true that the demand curve necessarily slopes downward and to the right. Or if it does, it doesn't necessarily always continue to slope to the right at any constant rate.

So Another Truth Bites the Dust

By now you should see that lowering the price does not necessarily mean you'll sell more. Products are bought and services are requisitioned, *not* because the price gets lower in many cases, but because of other things, including (as Chapter 19 discussed) quality, advertising, promotion, service, and ability to deliver the product.

23

We Can Sell Cheaper to the Large Quantity Buyer

Most marketing departments of most organizations believe that the large quantity buyer can justifiably be sold to at a lower price than the small quantity buyer, and that the marginal customer is a profitable customer. The reason for this, of course, is based on the belief that you have longer, more efficient production runs or that you are using an otherwise unused production capability in dealing with a large quantity buyer or a marginal customer. But much of the belief is that order entry, order processing, and order delivery are all a good deal less expensive with the quantity or marginal customer, and that therefore the customer who places a big or marginal order should receive some of the benefits and advantages of the "economies" that are realized as a result of the lesser activity required to handle and process their orders.

To be sure, processing a thousand orders to sell a thousand pounds is a good deal more expensive than processing one order to sell a thousand pounds. There's no argument with that idea. And the idea that the marginal customer contributes more than nothing is also true. The problem is in calculating *how much cheaper* you can really afford to sell. In other words, it's not the truth of the matter so much as it is *the degree of truth*.

Why It Won't Cost You Anything More

Large quantity and marginal buyers are very prone to lean on sales reps with the idea that "It won't really cost anything more if you sell this large order to me (or make this sale you otherwise wouldn't make), so I should receive all the savings that you will realize." This logic is hard to beat down by a sales rep because superficially it makes so much sense.

When the customer says, "Drop ship me three rail cars of such and such chemical," he's really saying, "You have the contact with the manufacturer but I have to place the order through you. All you've got to do is process the paperwork, the manufacturer ships directly to me, and you have no handling charges or any of the other attendant costs of doing business, so I want to realize the benefits of that."

Indeed, the same argument is often used on the manufacturer. "I'll give you a large quantity order. You gear up for a long production run. You plan your production schedules. You can buy from your suppliers in large quantities and get quantity discounts. You'll have fewer mistakes because your people will be doing the same thing over and over again. You'll have full machine and plant utilization advantages." And it always ends with the refrain, "...and you should pass the savings on to us."

But It Does Cost Something

While the refrain that it won't cost anything is constantly heard and superficially makes some sense, it really *does* cost something. What are some of the costs associated with that quantity or drop-shipped order? Well, for starters, it does take sales time, advertising, and promotion costs.

Sales Time, Advertising, and Promotion Costs

Negotiating a major purchase inevitably takes a long time. It isn't just here's the phone call and here's the order. It's here's an *inquiring* phone call. What can you do for us? Let's sit down and negotiate. And so the sales rep's time is expended fairly heavily in negotiating the lower price. And that means the general, selling, and administrative costs go up—especially the cost of selling.

In addition, other selling costs go up, too. Often there is the problem of samples, prototypes, contractual negotiations, meetings—all of which add to the general, selling, and administrative expenses. And frankly, those costs often are incurred in *greater* depth proportionate to the sales volume because of the haggling and negotiating that goes on over the "it won't cost you anything" logic.

Collection Costs Sometimes Go Up Too

There's always the chance that the quantity buyer will be a slow-pay customer. As pointed out in Chapter 20, the customer who is the most price sensitive is frequently the slowest to pay, doesn't have anyone in the office who can sign the checks, has the check in the mail but it must have gotten lost, etc. Invariably the customers to whom the price is the most dear are the ones who watch the dollars the closest. Because of that they tend to ride their suppliers financially by dragging out payables and otherwise inflicting on the supplier even more general and administrative costs—like telephone calls, collection fees, letters, computer printout on the dating of receivables, etc. So again, many of those customers who are totally price sensitive and who always look for the quantity deal may be the ones who are most apt to run up your general selling and administrative expenses on a disproportionate basis.

And You Must Process the Order Too

Don't forget, when the sale is made to that quantity or marginal buyer, the order must be processed. That means it has to be entered in the office, processed as the production goes on or the drop shipment arrangements made, followed up with invoicing and the usual customer-service-type expenses that are associated with customer-type businesses.

Also, when there are special order jobs of a large quantity basis, special requests often accompany them. It is not unusual for the customer to want one rail car to go to Houston, and another one to go to Dodge City, Kansas, and yet a third one to go to Birmingham. So the *one big order* is really *three smaller orders* in terms of routing and shipping procedures.

Over and beyond that there may be other associated special requests: special billing or packaging instructions, or information printed on the crates or boxes that the product is being shipped in. For some reason, the large quantity (discount) buyer seems to conveniently overlook the fact that the supplier's profit margin is lower and, inevitably, considers his firm to be a "preferred" customer who deserves special treatment.

Practically always added attention somehow becomes associated with the quantity order, if only because of the *unusualness* of the order itself. And different treatment means that the automatic machine designed and fine-tuned to process orders expeditiously and efficiently from an office gets disrupted because of the special order. And then personal care and attention in the hand carrying of documents, personal telephone calls and all related activity that goes on. And often it is not a clerk who can handle it—it has to be a vice president of marketing or perhaps even the president of the company who has to see to it that the unusually large order is handled "correctly." This distracts the executive from other time and activity necessary for running the business, and thus must also count toward running up administrative costs. Of course, it must be recognized that it's *only* the executive's time. And that executive doesn't really need to play golf, go jogging, or take a vacation. They really should work harder. But then they get executive burn-out, so here is another toll to extract.

So the idea that "it won't cost anything" simply is not true or defensible. It *does* cost something. In fact, it may cost more on a pro-rata basis instead of less when the general, selling, and administrative expenses of that special big order are considered.

The Usual Expenses Go On Anyway

General, selling, and administrative expenses are continually incurred, whether the firm's orders are large, medium, or small. And these expenses (which are *operating expenses* that do not relate directly to the *costs of producing or manufacturing* the product), are built up for some reason.

Officers' salaries are practically always included under the administrative salaries category, which also includes the salaries of people in the administrative or front offices. Somehow those people have to be there; and they have to be there for the little orders, the medium-sized orders, and the big and/or marginal orders, too. So, in distribution of costs, something must be attributed directly to those big and marginal orders.

The office also has to be there anyway. Our rent goes on, and if we didn't have the offices, we couldn't process the big order or the little orders. We also have repair and maintenance charges that have to be attributed to that major order the same as to the minor order. In addition to that, there may be all sorts of other GS&A expenses that must rightfully be attributed on some fair-share, pro-rata basis to that major order. The roof may begin to leak, the computer may break down, the city may assess the company for street improvements.

"Other" taxes have to be included as well as payroll taxes. Depreciation and deterioration charges against the office and administrative machinery and equipment must be attributed to that big order the same as any other order. Furthermore, interest costs must be attributed, and to some degree so must advertising and promotion costs, because large quantity and marginal order customers still had to find us and place that beneficial order with us.

How about employee benefits? Again, a pro-rata basis must be attributed to that large order customer for such things as pension and profit-sharing trust fund contributions, which may represent 15 percent of payroll. How about insurance coverage and medical and dental coverage for employees? All those need to be thrown in.

Then there is also the subject of office supplies and materials. Invoices must be printed up and mailed out. One invoice doesn't cost much, but it costs the same whether we're sending it to a large, marginal, or small buyer. And there are other office supplies—typewriter ribbons, printing and xerox charges, envelopes, erasers and paperclips and staples, dictating machines. And then, we must charge for telephone and postage, not to overlook the fact that we have accounting costs and data-processing costs directly attributable to that large order. In addition, legal fees may need to be tacked on because of the special nature of the contract that must be drawn up or perhaps because of legal problems in collecting for that large order.

The list continues. There may be such things as "other professional services" including consulting or memberships in professional organizations; and dues, subscriptions and/or licenses and fees to manufacture the product or distribute the product. Then, too, remember some of the "other selling" expenses to attribute to the one "big order" sale. Does the sales rep have to go make a call or two or ten on the major customer? And do we keep massaging the marginal customer's ego to get repeated big orders? Do we do more gifting and other benefiting and ego massaging activities for that major customer so that we can continue to reap their (low per-unit revenue) business? Even such things as our telephone charges can get extremely high because of the added "business promotional" activities we engage in trying to relate with that "big buying" customer.

On the face of it, it seems obvious that all those GS&A charges are going to be incurred whether the order is large or small. Admittedly, those costs of a big order aren't as high, but they *must* be counted. And, as pointed out, some costs are even increased because of the major order.

The pure and simple fact is that GS&A expenses are incurred as a result of all business operations. And business operations come about because orders are placed, whether they are large orders or small orders. And to suggest it won't cost anything, or very little, is to overlook the nature and fact of all those costs that are incurred. It doesn't just cost a little bit more; it may cost a lot more. It would take an extremely sharp pencil to calculate on a direct-cost basis exactly what those costs are, but they are probably a good deal more than the minimal amount attributed to them, particularly by the buyer who suggests it won't cost anything.

What Does It Cost To Fly in an Empty Airplane Seat?

Let's say an airplane is flying out and all the seats are not full. Any marketing genius can look at the fact that an airplane seat is empty and decide that any revenue generated from a pay-ing customer filling that last vacant seat is raw profit to the airlines. Right?

On the face of it, that's right. It costs the same amount to fly the airplane that distance; the extra 150 to 200 pounds of an extra paying customer simply doesn't raise operating costs at all. The airlines are well advised to board standbys who've paid anything for a ticket simply to fill that airplane up.

But if you're a frequent airline traveler, you'll know that's not true, because it *does* cost something to board that standby passenger. It takes a second or two longer to get that airplane departed because you have to load the standbys after you've loaded the airplane, and you've waited up until scheduled departure time to do that. So it takes a little extra time and a few extra minutes of the passenger agent's time. But that's real-ly only just a few pennies—well, maybe just a few dollars. It certainly is not anywhere near the value received from that plane fare of $50, $100, $200, $500, depending upon how long the trip is, right?

Wrong again, at least to some degree. What happens if, because of the standbys boarded, the plane arrives at its destination just a minute or so too late to make connections for other full-fare paying customers' baggage? So they go on to their final destinations without their baggage, which must be sent on separately to catch up with them. But that means the customer must file a lost baggage claim. More airlines person-nel will need to be available to take the baggage claim, which means more time will be spent tracing down where the lost baggage went, which in turn means more telephone calls within the organization. That also means calling up the customer and assuring him or her that the baggage is not totally lost and that it will arrive on tomorrow morning's plane.

When the baggage does arrive at the final destination for the full-fare paying customer, it must be delivered to the customer, who perhaps lives out on a farm 40 miles from town. That means freight and transportation charges, and payroll time for the driver to deliver it. Even when it's an in-town drop of a package or a bag, some costs will be incurred because some-body, be it a taxi-cab driver or a baggage/freight pool-delivery truck, has to deliver those bags to the full-fare paying customer. No matter how you slice it, that's expensive.

So it may well be that loading the standbys on the flight from Houston to Chicago ups the airline's revenues a few hundred dollars but, if all kinds of baggage misconnects in Chicago, it may cost a thousand dollars to cover just the lost baggage. So maybe 80 percent of the airplane passengers don't get their bags—or maybe 20 or 25 percent don't get their bags. If it costs only $50 per passenger in telephone calls, extra delivery charges, extra payroll time tracking down the baggage and filing the lost baggage report, and we lose 20 passengers' bags, then it has cost the airline $1,000 to board that standby passenger for that $100 ticket. This does not include the added expense of ill will from passengers who had to do without their luggage and the stress incurred by the airline employees who had to deal with the upset passengers.

Consider as well the "special deal" airline tickets designed to load the plane from 50 to 99 percent capacity. The people who are flying on the weekend specials, the thrift plans, the peanut fares, and the super-savers cost a whale of a lot to the airlines in terms of time and effort. Their tickets have to be issued, administrative overhead costs are continually incurred, cancellations and no-shows become problems, questions about "Will we be served lunch?" must be answered, service and maintenance must be pulled on the aircraft anyway, baggage must be checked, lost baggage retrieved, and on and on and on.

The facts are that even when discounts are offered to encourage people to fly, airlines inflict extra costs on themselves by pursuing discount strategies. When the airplane is full and running at full capacity, more snafus occur, more baggage gets lost, there's more need for additional last-minute boarding of meals to further delay departure and cause yet more misconnections (of both baggage *and* people), more safety cards need to be put on the airplane, additional toilet paraphernalia are used up, machinery and equipment are worn out faster, and customers get more irate—particularly *the full-fare paying business travelers* (who are so greatly inconvenienced that they begin to look for *alternative ways* to conduct business than by physically transplanting themselves from Houston to Chicago to Birmingham to Charlotte to Memphis to Cleveland to Chicago and back to Houston). "Maybe the telephone is an effective way to do business," they think, "or maybe a teleconferencing system or, better yet, a video teleconferencing system a la Buck Rogers and the space age makes more sense than transporting salespeople or executives all over the countryside."

Indeed, airlines seem to engage in a genocidal pursuit of the highest order in the limited amount of service (perhaps more accurately referred to as disservice) to the full-fare paying customer because they are galloping head-long into trying to fill airplanes with the logic that the empty airline seat will make profit dollars for the airlines if anybody will pay any kind of a price to sit in that seat.

But if indeed filling the empty airplane seat contributes directly to profitable operations for the airlines, then why is it true that in the late 1970s and early 1980s most airlines were operating unprofitably? And why did Braniff and Laker Airlines go bankrupt? The airlines tell us to blame it on the cost of jet fuel, but maybe a good deal of it has to do with "other expenses." Show me an airline whose major operating expense is fuel rather than labor.

And the Kicker Is...

The final kicker comes from looking at that airline example. What happens if we fill that last empty seat enough times? Invariably the marketing department decides they are doing such a good job of increasing demand for airline travel that they should add another flight and generate *yet more profit* for the airlines. When that last seat is filled and someone else comes up to the ticket counter who wants to fly, someone gets the bright idea that maybe we should have two nonstops a day rather than one. So another flight is added. But of course our competing airline also adds a flight, so we're right back to the old problem of flying airplanes with empty seats.

Well, there's a logical solution for that! Because those seats are not generating any revenue, let's discount the fares and get some people to sit in those seats and we'll fly those airplanes *full.* And then we'll really make some money. But then, again, what happens once we fill up those airplanes? We've got so much demand to fly on these routes we'd better add another flight. And when we add another flight, we then again have some empty seats. But that's easy to cope with. We'll just dis-

count some fares and fill up those empty seats and make a lot
more money.

If indeed the logic works, I would guess the airlines ought to
be even richer than the Arabs because they're making so much
money because they're filling all those seats with those
passenger discount fares "which don't cost anything and simply contribute profit dollars."

VI

*Truth in Production
and Finance*

24

Production Costs Decrease as Production Volume Increases

Anybody who has taken Econ 101 knows that when production volume is low, per-unit production costs are high and vice versa. Until a company realizes the *economies of scale* (which we all learned about in Econ 101), the costs of production will be high. Once those economies begin to materialize as production volume goes up, production costs will necessarily go down.

How To Paint a Room Efficiently, or Understanding Economies of Scale

Economies of scale begin as the production cycle becomes fine-tuned and volume increases. Then specialization helps to reap all the advantages and rewards of having specialists doing specialized jobs and doing them extremely efficiently. When everyone has a special job they do extremely efficiently, the per-unit costs of the increased volume of production go down.

I can remember when I first learned about this. The example that was used went like this: Assume that you want to paint your livingroom. You have to buy the paint, mix it, move all the furniture out of the room, put down drop cloths, get a step ladder, paint the room, clean the brushes and rollers, pick up the drop cloths, put the furniture back in the room, and generally rearrange things. Of course, working alone might cause some problems, like moving the heavy furniture, wasting time climbing up and down the step ladder to refill a paint bucket, driving back to the paint store for more paint, etc. In other words, working alone is not particularly efficient.

However, if you had a helper, you could send him or her to pick up the paint and mix it while you remove the small furniture from the room. Then your assistant could help you carry out the big stuff. And, while he or she puts down the drop cloths, you can get the step ladder and start painting. Your assistant could refill your paint bucket, and you could really hum along. If you were about to run out of paint, your assistant could anticipate this in the mixing process and run down to the store while you continued busily painting. Then, when you were finished painting, your assistant could help you move the furniture back in and all would be slick. The result of the two of you painting the room is that two people can paint the room in less than half the time that one person could paint the room. Now, you have begun to realize the *economies of scale*.

Suppose two friends come along to help you and your assistant. OK! Now you can really get organized and efficient. While your assistant goes and gets the paint and mixes, your two friends can remove the furniture from the room and you can be putting the drop cloths down and getting out the step ladder. As soon as your assistant returns with the paint, you and your two friends can start painting, and your assistant can supply all three of you with the necessary paint. Should you begin to run low on paint, your assistant can run down to the paint shop while one of your friends continues to feed paint to the two of you who continue painting. When it is all over, one person can pick up the drop cloths, two people can bring in the heavy furniture, and one can bring in the light furniture, and behold, the four of you have painted the room in less than one-quarter of the time that it would have taken you to do it yourself.

So goes the idea of economies of scale. Now to be sure, this cannot keep on forever. Obviously, if a hundred of your closest friends drop by there may be a little problem of duplication of effort, people getting in each other's way, somebody spilling the paint, or somebody getting mad. So you can get too much of a good thing. Anybody knows that.

But within some bounds of reason, economies of scale can be worked out quite well, and you can get far more efficient by increasing your volume of production. Therefore, we have shown again that production costs go down as production volume goes up because you get more efficient.

And So It Is True in the World

Take this example and apply it to the real world. What you get is known as production efficiency, or specialization, or fine-tuning a production operation, or truth. *Fact:* Your production costs go down as your production volume goes up—so long as you don't overextend the basic principle and reach the point of diminishing returns.

Unfortunately, some pretty solid statistics show this is folly.

The Shooter's Bible

All industries have a set of facts and figures collected by some agency to monitor what goes on. We have, for example, amassed figures from day one in the baseball record books. We know how many times Babe Ruth struck out, how many hits Ty Cobb had, how many home runs Ralph Kiner hit, how many walks Grover Cleveland Alexander gave up (as well as the statistics about the other records they accumulated).

This seems to be done in all sports. Somebody keeps the books and records. Those books and records become bibles. And so it seems in business. Somebody keeps the books. And the book that is the authority—so to speak, the "Shooter's Bible" of industry statistics—is the Annual Statement Studies compiled by Robert Morris Associates in Philadelphia.*

This book is an on-going collection of information that presents a composite look at the financial data of U.S. com-

---

* Robert Morris Associates, *1980 Annual Statement Studies* (Philadelphia: Robert Morris Associates), 1980.

panies. This is *the* book that most bankers refer to if they want a good inside view of how your business's operations compare to other businesses in industries like your own. This is the book that your banker may refer to in making a judgment call as to whether or not you are a loan-worthy applicant, whether or not your line of credit should be extended, whether or not your note should be called, whether or not, in short, your business is worth a damn.

If you read the 1980 Annual Statement Studies published by Robert Morris Associates (the only reason I pick on that issue is that it's the most recent at the time of this writing) you will find that in fact in 82.4 percent of the manufacturing industries reported on, manufacturing costs as a percentage of sales go *up* as sales volume grows—rather than going down, which is the reverse of what TRUTH tells us!

What? It can't be so! Say it isn't so.

Yes, it is so. By actual count, for 82.4 percent of the manufacturing industries reported on in the 1980 study, when companies are very small their manufacturing costs as a percentage of their sales are *as low or lower than* when the companies get larger. The statistics show that of the 131 manufacturing industries reported on:

1. In 84 out of the 131, production costs as a percentage of sales definitely went *up* as the sales volume of the companies increased.
2. In 24 of the 131, there was no evidence of any change, but costs definitely did *not* go down as the sales volume of the companies increased.
3. In only 23 of the 131 (17.6 percent of the total) did production costs go down as production volume went up.

But how can this be so? My economics prof said that production costs go down as production volume goes up.

Well, OUR Per-Unit
Production Costs Have Gone Down

Doubtless some business managers have indeed seen their production costs decrease as their volume increased. This was accomplished by building new plants that were far more efficient, and they *know* for a fact that their per-unit production costs have gone down.

There are two responses to this. One, they may be among the fortunate 17.6 percent whose per-unit production costs actually *do* go down while production volume goes up and their sales volume grows in their business. That, of course, is entirely possible and I can't deny it happens. In some cases, production costs *do* go down.

But the other answer may well be that while per-unit production costs have gone down, *production costs as a percentage of sales nevertheless have gone up*, the lower production costs notwithstanding.

The problem comes from the fact that we always overbuild plant capacity and, because we have excess capacity and we "know" that our production costs will go down as our production volume goes up, we are tempted to bid down the selling price of our products in order to get the volume necessary to fill up our new, modern, more efficient plant.

And when we start bidding down the price we sell our product for, we seemingly always (or at least in 82.4 percent of the cases) bid our prices down lower than what our reduced production costs are and, on a relative basis, our production costs as a *percentage* of our selling price actually go up. Thus, while our production costs have gone down, our sales revenues have gone down more rapidly. Put another way, as our production costs per unit go down, our sales price per unit goes down more rapidly. So, by default, our production costs go up as our production volume increases. And the problem with that is—profitability goes to hell!

This phenomenon is partly explained by studies of business profitability related to business size. Return on assets and return on net worth in the larger businesses are inevitably lower than they are for all but the very smallest businesses.*

---

* To thoroughly research this statement, see H.O. Stekler, *Profitability and Size of the Firm* (Berkeley, Calif: University of California Institute of Business and Economic Research), 1963. For more recent data see John H. Sheridan, "Is There Still Room for the Little Guy?" *Industry Week* (Sept. 15, 1975), pages 30–41. Also, for current data see any of the annual business performance figures of such magazines as *Fortune* or *Business Week*.

This also accounts for the phenomenon that it is not unheard of for companies who get into financial trouble to raise their prices, lower their sales volume, and *increase* profitability. By default, they actually are able to lower their production costs per unit (relative to prices) by cutting back on their volume of production relative to their selling price. They may lose the marginal price-buying customer, but they gain gross margin and therefore profitability by cutting back on their volume of sales.

Complications: That Empty Seat on the Airplane

Suppose we have a manufacturing plant. When we really get humming, our per-unit production costs can actually go down—for the moment we'll consider that a fact. So we "know" that if we can generate more sales volume, we can make more profit. So we go out and beat the bushes to generate additional sales—not unlike the airline offering discounts to otherwise reluctant travelers. And we fill our plant (or airplane) with reluctant buyers, but buyers who are induced to buy from us because our price is "more competitive."

So now we fill our plant up and we poke our heads up, look around, and say to ourselves, "Hey, we need an *even bigger* plant. We're about to bust at the seams with all this new business volume coming in." So we decide to build a new *more efficient* plant (like buying another airplane—but a bigger and better one). Now we build our new plant. But when we build the new plant, we always build in some excess capacity, because we know we are going to "grow" and "while we're at it, we may as well do it right."

We move into our new plant, get all the bugs out and get everything set up. But now we're only running at 40 percent of the plant's capacity. Our graduates from Econ 101 look around and say, "Hey, if we could get a little more volume in here we could get our production costs down to where we're really operating at an efficient rate and really make more money." So we lean on the sales force to pound the bushes to get more business. Of course the best way to do that is to attract that marginal (price-buying) customer. And the way to get the marginal customer is to bid the price down. (Maybe we can even get someone who will give us a super-large quantity order.

After all, as is pointed out in Chapter 23, we can sell cheaper to the large quantity buyer because it doesn't really cost anything to add that extra volume.)

So now we fill up our plant with our lower price business. Our gross margin goes to hell again, but our plant is full. And we're *really* humming. Besides that, if we could just increase our volume a little bit more with a more efficient plant we could really make some profit. We are busting at the seams in our "old" new plant. But, after all, we're in a growth industry, and we're certainly doing a good job. Look at all the sales volume increases that we've had. The demand is out there for our product. Look at our track record. Maybe we better build a new plant. We could build a *really good* new plant. One that is really modern and efficient and has lots of capacity. So let's do that.

We build another new plant. But now our new plant is only running at 40 percent of capacity. So maybe we better fill it up with business so we can really get the benefit of those economies of scale. Let's just lean on the sales force to get some new sales. And the ongoing spiral continues.

We All Believe in the Bottom Line

What we're trying to pursue, after all, is more profit. We're trying to increase "the bottom line." Our fixed costs and plant operations spur us on to increasing volume, but the only way we can get the required volume is by bidding down the price. And then our margins go to hell, and we get ourselves on a treadmill.

All we wanted was to grow, get bigger, expand. And what happened was, while realizing efficiencies in our new modern plants, we built *yet more* new modern plants, which put us back on the inefficient side of production operations.

Maybe we can best visualize this by looking at the following charts. When production volume is relatively low, production costs per unit are relatively high. However, as we begin to increase production volume and realize those wonderful economies of scale, we can get our per-unit production costs down. As we all learned in Econ 101, usually a production cost curve is a reverse J shape, shown in the first graph.

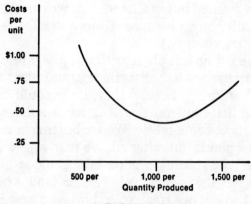

FIGURE 24-1

Now we begin to increase our production volume, and we get more efficient. But we also fill up our plant, because we want to make more money. So we need to build a new, more modern, more efficient plant. Looking at time-series data, we impose on ourselves a new production cost curve once we get our new plant. This can be seen in the second graph.

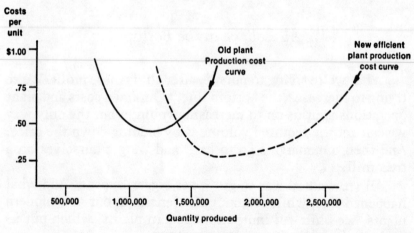

FIGURE 24-2

It shows that when we open our new plant, we have a new marginal cost curve. It is true, of course, that our whole per-unit production cost curve is lower, reflecting our more efficient plant. But, unfortunately, by building more capacity than we need, we are still on the left-hand side of our production

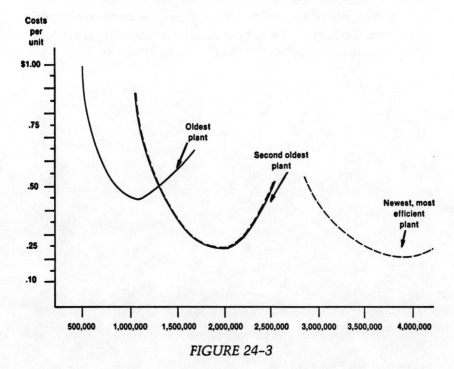

FIGURE 24-3

cost curve, which is high. So, to fill our plant and get to the point where we're really producing efficiently at production, we try to sell more. But then we fill up that plant and we build a new one. Now, we have the situation illustrated in the third graph.

The same problem occurs with our third plant as with our second plant. Yet there's no denying the fact that our per-unit production costs have gone down. We are more efficient. But, to develop the sales volume necessary to fill this third plant to its "efficient" capacity, we have to again bid our price down. And that is why the Robert Morris Associates statistics are true: Our per-unit production costs do go down as our production volume goes up, but if our per-unit selling price goes down *even further,* our per-unit production costs relative to our selling price *actually increase,* and it becomes progressively difficult to increase profitability.

This is what happens to many U.S. industries today. And this is why studies of business profitability show that inevitably, while making more dollars of profit, large-volume manufacturers make less profit dollars in terms of their return on investment. Historically, this seems to always be the case and, given the nature of business and the number of people who take Econ 101, it may well continue to be true.

25

What Counts
Is the Bottom Line

I wish I had a nickel for every time I heard a business manager
or executive say "What counts is the bottom line." It refers to,
of course, the end result, the *final product*, what's left over
after all the dust settles, the remains.

This overwhelming concern with the bottom line implies
that the action in between is of little interest. It is the end
result alone that counts. Is there a profit? Is there any money
left to be taken out of the business? Was it worth going through
all the exercise of running the business, buying materials,
processing them through production operations, advertising
them for sale through retail and wholesale operations, paying
all the help in the office, paying the utility bills, insurance,
advertising, and so on? We're in business for the bottom line.
And if there isn't something left over to make it all worthwhile, why mess with it?

Gonna Break a Million

Everyone *knows* that what's important is the bottom line,
but very few people actually behave that way. In fact, it would
appear that what they're interested in is the *top* line.

The bottom line shows profit dollars. The top line shows
the size of your empire, how major a competitor you are in the
marketplace, how much activity you have, how many people

report to you, the vastness of your management talents—in short, the top line shows the world that you've got your act together.

If you've ever been to a managerial or executive training program you remember the introductions of each attendee. Usually they go like this:

"Hi, I'm Arnold Falls from Nester Stye, Colorado. We're located in a suburb of Denver. We make electronic parts. I started my business four years ago. The first year, sales were only $150,000, but we doubled in the second year to $300,000, and in the third year we hit almost $600,000. This year we expect to break a million."

Arnold Falls' introduction is followed by the individual sitting on Arnold's left whose name is Anthony Lopez. Anthony's introduction runs like this:

"Uh, I'm Anthony Lopez. My business is located in the outskirts of Houston. We manufacture computer software. I started my business ten years ago and we're currently doing $2.8 million in sales. Our business is pretty good. While profitability hasn't been as high as we had hoped, our growth rate has been fantastic. I'm glad to be here, and I hope I learn a lot from this program."

After Anthony finishes, he's followed by the individual on his left, Sally Fenster. Her introduction runs as follows:

"My name is Sally Fenster. I'm with Dog Wallow, Inc. We make dog houses and other high-quality housing for animals. My husband and I started the business two years ago. Our sales haven't been all that spectacular, but we're currently doing $600,000 in sales. The reason is that we started a new line of products for housing cattle. We hope to break a million this year and our current sales rate is projected actually to be almost $1,100,000 by the end of our fiscal year. We've had a lot of fun running the business, and we hope to grow quite a lot over the next several years."

The introductions go on and on. Sometimes the companies are bigger. "Hi, I'm Johnny Jones and we sell processed meat. We currently do about $25 million in sales. Our growth has been spectacular. In the next five years we expect to reach something like $50 million."

While the size may change, one unalterable truth does not. Everybody talks about how *fast* they're growing and how *big* they're getting—because being big means that you have size, power, control, a vast empire, and proven worth in the marketplace. But it also means what you're really interested in is the top line, *not the bottom line.*

You hardly ever hear anyone come to a program and say something to the effect of, "Hi, my name is Bill Smith. We make lots of money. We're not too big in sales. We only do an annual volume of about $375,000, but our net profit is $221,000, after I take a salary of $100,000 plus a company car. We're only interested in making money. We don't want to get bigger."

Once in a while you hear someone say, "We are highly profitable." But usually they talk about size, because that describes what they're *really* worth.

After One Comes Two,
Then Five—and It All Starts Over Again

The top line always seems to be measured in a series of 1, 2, 5, and then the cycle starts all over again.

Those who run businesses that are "just under a million" in sales have an intense need to break a million. Once they break a million, the next target is to break 2 million in sales. But once they break 2 million in sales, then they have to set their cap for 5 million in sales.

With due diligence, perseverence, and hard work, they can break 5 million in sales. After that, they have to look up to see what's next—because the sequence starts all over again and runs 1, 2, and 5, with a zero behind each number. Since the numbers you put after it are in the millions, what you say is "We hope to break 10 million." Of course, once you break 10 million, you've got to break 20 million. After you've broken 20 million, then you've got to break 50 million.

Unfortunately, it doesn't stop then. Once the organization has grown to 50 million, the next target is the big one—100 million. After 100 million, 200 million is surely the real action, so breaking 200 million becomes the goal. This is usually accomplished by acquisition and merger, because it's awfully hard to take nothing (i.e., 100 million in sales) and build it into 200 million in sales. Suddenly, after breaking 200 million, 500 million begins to have a nice ring to it. You can pronounce it "one half billion."*

Which Do You Want to Be—Big or Profitable?

The problem is that altogether too often the pursuit of getting bigger destroys profitability. H.O. Stekler years ago did a study of profitability and company size.** He found that as companies got much over about $10 million in sales, their rate of profitability (return on investment) began to decrease. And this seems to hold true today, including companies over $100 million in sales size.

According to research done in the early 1960s by Clare Griffin, Professor Emeritus of the University of Michigan's Graduate School of Business, the three primary goals of presidents of the Fortune 500 companies, in order of frequency of mention and importance, were:
1. Growth
2. Share of market
3. Profitability

If that remains true (and I am sure it is), large and small companies in the United States have been driven for 20 years by the desire to get bigger. Everybody wants to get bigger and dominate the industry; everybody wants an increasing share of the market; everybody wants to grow. But what we believe in is the bottom line. Ask whomever you have lunch with today....

Getting bigger doesn't necessarily mean losing profitability. But getting bigger usually means loss of profitability. Not in absolute dollars, but in rate of return on investment. So getting bigger must be more important than maintaining profitability;

---

* I can tell you for a fact about the day I sat in corporate headquarters of a $700 million corporation and listened to the president of that company tell his executive cadre, "Ladies and gentlemen, we are currently doing just at $700 million in annual sales volume. I expect to see us break $1 billion in sales prior to the time of my retirement." Lots of hand clapping. Everybody knew that they were in a corporate giant's office. I didn't have guts enough to ask what came after 1 billion. My suspicion is 2 billion. In fact, I'd be willing to put money on it.

** loc. cit.

otherwise companies wouldn't be stampeded into constantly striving to expand, enlarge, or increase their market share and market position.

Gonna Break Ten Million

In 1981 I had a client who in 1979 did just around $7 million in sales. In 1979 he had the dream to break "the big one"—$10 million. So he launched a strong campaign to get bigger. His business was wholesale distribution, and his financial statement for 1979 (figures rounded) looked like this:

Sales	$7,000,000
Cost of goods sold	5,460,000
Gross margin	$1,540,000
Operating expenses:	
Fixed expenses	900,000
Variable expenses	430,000
Net profit	$ 210,000

Now, calculating the profit percentage on sales, you can see that the net profit percentage on sales was exactly 3 percent. And for the nature of this business, that was considered okay—not great, but okay in terms of profit percentage on sales.

Using some of the logic from Chapter 21, the breakeven volume for this business in 1979 calculates out to $5,660,377.30. The mathematics work as follows:

$$\text{Breakeven volume} = \frac{\text{Fixed operating expenses}}{\text{Gross margin percentage} - \text{Variable expense percentage}}$$

Plugging in the numbers it looks as follows:

$$\text{Breakeven volume} = \frac{\$900,000}{.22 - .061}$$

$$\text{Breakeven volume} = \frac{\$900,000}{.159}$$

$$\text{Breakeven volume} = \$5,660,377.30$$

Calculating that breakeven volume, this business broke even at roughly 81 percent of the annual volume of sales of $7 million (which they realized in 1979).

For a wholesale distribution business, this appears okay. No consultant would have been particularly alarmed at these financial ratios.

But We're Going to Grow

But the owner of this business decided that $7 million in sales with adequate profits was not sufficient. Because what counts is the bottom line, and the way you increase the bottom line is to increase sales volume.

In 1980 the company realized a 20-percent sales increase by becoming far more price competitive (one of the better ways to grow is to cut your price).*

So in 1980 the company became price competitive, and their sales volume began to grow. Furthermore, supplementing their price competitiveness, they also began to give away free goods as incentives to their customers to place larger orders with them. In addition, given the state of the economy in 1980, they began to offer rebates and discounts to customers for volume purchases. Then they began to give their customers dating (the practice of shipping to them now, but giving them a date later in the year when the account becomes payable).

All of these competitive devices designed to enhance sales are just another way of saying, "We're cutting prices." Free goods given to retailers as incentives to buy from the wholesaler simply gives that retailer more goods to resell and represents a price discount. Necessarily, rebates and discounts represent a lower price, and dating does too, because you lose the use of money that you would otherwise have had during the extended period.

Furthermore, in an effort to become extremely price competitive, this wholesale distributor did more institutional

---

* Of course, as is pointed out in Chapter 21, you can't make any money because you can't make it up in volume. But if you hadn't read Chapter 21 and hadn't read this chapter yet, you might still believe that one of the better ways to grow is to become price competitive.

advertising, thereby running up his fixed expenses some $200,000. Not all of this, of course, had to do with added promotion. A lot of it had to do with the added office help necessary because sales volume had increased by 20 percent, necessitating increases in the number of invoices processed and sent out, record keeping, accounting costs, payroll dollars, office machinery and equipment, postage costs, etc.

Therefore, in 1980, compared to 1979, the financial statement looked like the following:

	1979	1980
Sales	$7,000,000	$8,400,000
Cost of goods sold	5,460,000	6,636,000
Gross margin	$1,540,000	$1,764,000
Operating expenses:		
Fixed expenses	$ 900,000	$1,100,000
Variable expenses	430,000	$ 504,000
Net profit	$ 210,000	$ 160,000

As we said, the breakeven volume in 1979 was when the business was doing 81 percent of its annual volume. If we calculate it for 1980, it works as follows:

$$\text{Breakeven volume} = \frac{\$1,100,000}{.21 - .06}$$

$$\text{Breakeven volume} = \frac{\$1,100,000}{.15}$$

$$\text{Breakeven volume} = \$7,333,333.33$$

That breakeven volume represents 87 percent of the annual sales volume in 1980. Any consultant would be slightly concerned about how this business was functioning, because the net profit percentage had slipped from .03 in 1979 to .02 in 1980. Furthermore, the breakeven volume was getting dangerously close to the annual sales volume—and exceeded the previous year's sales volume in dollars.

We're Gonna Kill 'Em

In 1981 they really got serious at cutting prices and increasing volume. They began to offer more free goods, rebates, discounts, and dating.

And they also began to be hammered by pressure from the bigger customers to drop ship. The logic, of course, from the bigger customers was, "It really doesn't cost anything to add our extra volume because we're such a large quantity buyer. You can give us a better price." The owner apparently didn't know about the logic of empty airplane seats costing money when they get filled. In fact, he just looked at the drop-ship price and figured that all they had to do was tack on a few percentage points above their own cost and they would certainly make it up in volume.

And sales did grow—to the $10,500,000 mark. "Yippee, we did it!! We broke $10 million! Let's put a new chart on the wall." But while their sales volume increased, their gross margin decreased because of their price cutting and wheeling and dealing. Something else happened, also: their fixed operating expenses climbed—fairly dramatically—by $420,000.

Why did this happen? Because now, in two years' time, they had a total growth rate of 56* percent over the previous two years. ("We must be doing something right with that kind of growth rate.") And because their growth rate was so high, they found that their office facilities simply were not suited to handle the extra volume that they were realizing. It became necessary to find new office space and that cost a little money. Plus, the "while we're at its" began to get them. "While we're at it, let's put in the right furniture and fixtures, machinery and equipment in the office. While we're at it, we simply *must* have a computer. Because you can't run a $10 million business without a computer. And we may as well get a good one while we're at it. Because we're going to continue to grow. After all, our growth rate has been 56 percent over the past two years. Why, in another two or three years we'll probably be breaking $20 million the way things are going."

*Figured on cost of goods sold.

So their operating expenses went up. And 1981, compared to 1979 and 1980, looked like this:

	1979	1980	1981
Sales	$7,000,000	$8,400,000	$10,500,000
Cost of goods sold	5,460,000	6,636,000	8,505,000
Gross margin	$1,540,000	$1,764,000	1,995,000
Operating expenses:			
Fixed expenses	$ 900,000	$1,100,000	$ 1,520,000
Variable expenses	430,000	$ 504,000	609,000
Net profit	$ 210,000	$ 160,000	($ 134,000)

Calculating the breakeven point is academic at this point. Obviously they lost $134,000 from operations. But the breakeven looks as follows:

$$\text{Breakeven volume} = \frac{\$1,520,000}{.19 - .058}$$

$$\text{Breakeven volume} = \frac{\$1,520,000}{.132}$$

$$\text{Breakeven volume} = \$11,515,151$$

Their breakeven volume occurred at 109.6 percent of their actual volume. In short, they would have broken even in their thirteenth month. Unfortunately, like the rest of us, they only had 12 months in their accounting period for that year.

Doctors and Nurses Cannot Put Scrambled Eggs Back into the Shell

The long and short of this is that everybody *believes* in the bottom line, but what they try to increase is the top line.

This is not to argue that growth is not good. Profitable growth *is* good. The problem is that we assume profitability will automatically accompany growth, which isn't always the case. In fact, statistics show that once a business gets much over about $10 million in sales, profitability begins to decrease relative to the funds and efforts invested in the business.

But, somehow, to be bigger just seems better. Growth is what counts. Command and control can come only from size and power. It's the American way. So we'll pay lip service to the bottom line, but what we'll try to do is increase the top line.

But I would recommend that any executive in a command position in any U.S. organization rethink this fundamental question: Which do you want to be, big *or* profitable? And then consider this question: Are you *really* running your business to achieve that goal?

26

We Can Finance
Our Growth from Earnings

Some executives believe that their company can finance their growth from earnings. Believing this is very much akin to believing the person who steps into your office and says: "I'm from the government and I'm here to help you."

In truth, it is very unlikely that your business is prosperous enough to finance its growth from its earning power. Very few are. It is highly unlikely that, if you're in the manufacturing, wholesale/distribution, or retailing business, you will be able to finance your growth from earnings. The odds are a good deal better if you're in the service or construction business.

How Much Money
Is Needed to Finance Growth?

One question I am often asked by executives is, "How much money will we need to finance our growth over the coming X number of years?" The answer to that question can be a very complex, involved relationship. I could answer that question with questions: How rapid is your growth rate? How much money do you expect to take out in dividends paid to stockholders? What is your business's borrowing capacity? How much will your customers be willing to carry you for extended terms? Are you a front money business? What is your debt-to-worth ratio? What is your quick ratio? What are your earnings before interest and taxes? What has been your record concerning retained earnings over the past several years? What kind of depreciation schedule have you been using on your building, your machinery, your equipment? How much money do you have tied up in inventories? How quickly does inventory turn over? How slow paying are your accounts receivable? How good are your accounts receivable? Is there any way you can expedite collection of your receivables? Is there any way you can slow down the purchase of inventory? What is the age and condition of your primary machinery and equipment? And so on.

These are difficult questions. But there is a simple formula that is uncannily accurate in predicting how much cash a company will need to finance its growth. And it can be summarized as follows:

$$\left[\frac{\text{Expected sales increase}}{\frac{\text{Last year's sales}}{\text{Last year's total average assets}}} \right] = \text{Required financing for growth}$$

- Depreciation schedule for coming year net of loan principle repayments
- Expected retained earnings for coming year
- Investment tax credit for coming year
= Cash shortfall if a positive number

According to this formula you need to know the following information to calculate the amount of money your business will need to finance its growth:

1. The expected growth rate for the coming period (presumably a year).
2. Last year's net sales volume.
3. Last year's total average asset base.
4. The expected amount of money from earnings for the coming year, which will be left in the business after all year-end "adjustments" have been made and all taxes have been paid.
5. Expected depreciation to be applied against assets for the coming year, net of loan principle repayments.
6. Any investment tax credits expected to be applied for the coming year.

These six items are all you need to find your business's growth requirements. One other item will add a little refinement—or, more likely, a little cold water to be thrown on the best of plans. That factor is the *amount of equity* found in the business.

Expected Growth Rate for the Year

The expected growth rate for the coming period is important information for us. Normally we plan on an annual basis, so we'll be concerned here, for purposes of developing our formula, with next year's expected growth rate.

Most managerial planners who have the task of developing financial data concerning a business's growth think primarily in terms of percentage increases or dollar-sales volume increases expected in the coming year. This figure can be obtained from a realistic sales or marketing forecast projected by the firm. Say, for example, that our business has been doing $10 million in sales during the past year, and we expect to realize a 25-percent increase in dollar-sales volume, or a $2,500,000 increase in total net sales for the coming year.

Note: We do not need to know, nor can we effectively use, the expected sales increase in *units* of sales, because our cash needs are essentially going to be tied to inflation. We need to know our dollar-sales volume increase, because we will have to buy and finance that expected dollar-sales volume increase with inflated dollars as the year progresses. Thus, we must think in pragmatic terms, i.e., the amount of money that will *actually* be required, not the percentage increase in unit of sales. Even if *all* the expected dollar-sales increase comes from inflation and none comes from an increase in unit sales, our expected dollar-sales increase must still be used, because our cash needs will increase the next year even if we sold no additional units. This assumes that our costs for inventory, material, labor, etc. will inflate as *our* price increases inflate our sales volume. Once we have ascertained what we think our dollars-of-sales increase will be for the coming year, we then need to determine last year's net sales volume.

Last Year's Net Sales Volume

Determining last year's net sales volume should be relatively easy. Our accountant can give us that information shortly after fiscal year-end close. This need only be a closely approximated figure; in fact, preliminary closing figures are more than adequate. Assume, for sake of example, that last year's net sales figure was $10 million, which was the figure used to project our 25-percent increase in net dollar sales for the coming year in the foregoing section.

Last Year's Net Average Asset Base

The next thing which we need to know is the total average asset base that we operated on last year. This figure is obtainable from the year-end close balance sheet under the heading of "total assets." Again, an exact figure is not necessary; only a good close guesstimate is required.

Here what we're looking for is the total number of dollars tied up in assets, which will tell us approximately the total sum of money that must be invested to generate the required sales volume. (Note: Assets should be considered on an average basis where inventory and accounts receivable are concerned. This figure will give the average total value of monies tied up in all forms of assets used to generate the sales volume, which we have been experiencing in our most recent year of operation.)

Let us assume that our company is a manufacturing company. And, typical of most manufacturing firms, our net sales volume runs about twice our total asset base as carried on the books. Therefore, we will assume for our example that the total average asset value for our business is about five million dollars at depreciated value.

Required Financing for Growth

The total sum of money required to finance the growth can be calculated by taking our expected dollar-sales volume increase and dividing it by the dividend of last year's net sales figure, divided by last year's total average asset base at depreciated value. The quotient will tell us the total sum of money required to finance our expected growth in sales for the coming year.

Putting it into our formula, it looks as follows:

$$\dfrac{\$\ 2{,}500{,}000}{\left[\begin{array}{c}\$10{,}000{,}000 \\ \$\ 5{,}000{,}000\end{array}\right]} = \$1{,}250{,}000$$

If we are going to increase our sales volume by $2,500,000, we will probably need $1,250,000 in financing in order to support that growth. Believe it or not, this simple formula will pretty accurately tell us how much money we will need. And the reason is because it simply says that *the relationship between sales and assets in a business tends to hold constant*. Therefore, because last year's net sales and last year's total average assets at depreciated value ran at a rate of two times sales to one times assets, if we expect an increase in sales volume of $2,500,000, our asset base will probably have to grow by one-half that figure. Thus, our asset base will have to increase by approximately $1,250,000, thereby maintaining the same relationship we've historically had.

We Can Always Produce More
Without Increasing Our Asset Base Significantly

Most people can understand the mathematics involved in determining how much cash is needed to finance the growth, but they choose to *deceive* themselves in managing their businesses by *erroneously* believing that they can increase their sales volume fairly significantly *without* substantially increasing their asset base. They think they can put on a second shift (or simply run more traffic through the store, if they are retailers) instead, without adding any additional assets.

Certainly, manufacturers can add a second shift or can begin working their plant overtime; retailers can run more people through the store. By doing so, they *can* utilize their fixed assets—land, building, machinery, and equipment. But fixed assets for the typical manufacturer (or for any business for that matter) are usually the *smallest* (and in many cases an inconsequential amount) of the total assets found in a business.

For example, the typical manufacturer who has an asset base of one-half net sales (as we established before) will find that that asset base is usually composed primarily of two items more significant than land, building, machinery, and equipment. Those items are *receivables and inventories.*

The largest percentage of assets is usually tied up in inventories: raw materials, work in process, finished goods inventory, demonstration inventory, etc. As the production function is increased, increased value is added to raw materials in the form of wages and other production costs as inventories are built up for final sale and shipment.

Accounts receivable also take up a large percentage of the total asset base. In fact, it is not unusual to see inventories and receivables amount to 60–80 percent of the total asset base of any given manufacturer. And the irrefutable truth is that as sales volume goes up, inevitably inventories and receivables *also go up on a dollar-for-dollar, pro-rata basis.* Face the facts: the bulk of the manufacturer's assets simply go up on a pro-rata basis with sales because inventories and accounts receivable are tied to sales volume.

For those involved in retailing, wholesaling, service, and construction industries, the same facts hold true, because the wholesaler or retailer's inventories and receivables practically always increase every bit as fast as sales. It is imperative for retailers to have inventories in stock to generate sales volume required. In fact, for many retailers their inventories climb *more* rapidly than their sales volume. This fact is also true for many wholesalers.

So it may be true that your sales base can be increased to some extent more rapidly than assets—but it depends on what your fixed-asset base is relative to your total assets. If your fixed assets are a fairly small percentage of your total assets, it is futile to even argue the point; if they are a major portion of your total assets, then you may have some point (that is, assuming that you have a *lot of excess* capacity in your fixed assets). But most manufacturers, retailers, wholesalers, and service industry and construction types run at or as near to peak capacity as possible for their fixed assets. It only makes good economic sense. The truth is (as pointed out in Chapter 23), most businesses try to operate at the economic quantity that gives them relatively *fully* utilized fixed assets. And once you get somewhere close to pushing capacity, you always build a bigger, better, more modern, more efficient plant (or store or warehouse). This inevitably causes a significant increase in your fixed-asset base, which means that your fixed-asset base does not progress in a smooth, even flow over the years, but tends to rise in quantum jumps.

For *most* industries, the total asset base, relative to sales, actually *increases* as a percentage of sales rather than decreases. According to the Robert Morris Associates figures,* in the manufacturing industry, as the business sales volume increases, sales to total assets actually stay the same or *decrease* in 91 percent of the cases; sales to total assets increase in only 9 percent of the cases. Similar figures for wholesalers show that sales to total assets stay the same or go down in 86 percent of the cases, while in only 14 percent of the cases do they go up. Likewise, in retailing, the sales to assets either stay the same or go down 82 percent of the time; those that increase are 18 percent. Figures in the service and construction industry show that the relationship between sales and assets stay the same or go down in 92 percent of the cases, while those that go up do so 8 percent of the time.

There simply is no justification to argue that a business is apt to grow without increasing its asset base as quickly as sales. In fact, in the overwhelmingly large majority of the cases, the asset base for the firm will increase *more rapidly* rather than more slowly. So whichever industry you're in, you're going to have to accept the first portion of the formula. Your expected sales increase can be divided by your historical sales-to-asset ratio to give you a pretty good approximation of the amount of money you will need to finance your growth. And this is a conservative figure—conservative in the sense that the sales-to-asset ratio declines for most businesses, indicating that *more* money will be needed rather than less. Using last year's basic ratio is sufficient in most cases to determine the amount of money required to finance the growth of the business.

---

* Robert Morris Associates 1980 *Annual Statement Studies.*

230 TRUTH IN PRODUCTION AND FINANCE

How Much Money
Can Our Business Provide for Our Growth?

Once the amount of money required to finance the growth of the firm is determined, we can deduct from that our firm's earnings capability to provide for that required financing. The second portion of the formula shows that we subtract from our required financing for growth the net earnings capability (in after-tax dollars for the coming year), the expected depreciation schedule for the coming year, and any investment tax credits we expect to realize.

Expected After-Tax
Retained Earnings for the Coming Year

First, subtract the amount of money that you expect to earn after taxes and be able to leave in the business for the coming year's operations—this means earnings that are left to be used in the business *after* making all the year-end "adjustments" and after paying all year-end taxes that will be due. These "adjustments" can be significant, and this figure should not be confused with either pre-tax or after-tax net profit, if expenditures such as pension or profit-sharing contributions, dividends, bonuses, etc. have not been deducted.

Many U.S. corporations appear to try to minimize taxes *after* they've tried to maximize profitability (a debatable point, but we'll say it anyway; see Chapter 25).

In most U.S. corporations, monies that can be made are made; then, with an eye toward the IRS, those legal "adjustments" are made at the end of the year, designed to minimize our tax bite. Such things as making contributions to the pension and profit-sharing trust funds are, of course, an opener. Over and beyond that, bonuses are given to key employees to keep them motivated. We may also make some contributions to various other organizations and agencies that seem appropriate. Furthermore, in anticipation of having a good year, we may commit to a few other expenses for remodeling, refurbishing, replacing, or modernizing operations. After all, we're paying for it with half the money coming from Uncle Sam. because we're avoiding taxes. Then, too, maybe the shareholders deserve some dividends.

These year-end "adjustments" are perfectly legal and constantly practiced. There's only one problem with them: while we pay for them with half the government's money, we also pay with *half the company's money!* The facts are that when we make a donation to the pension and profit-sharing trust fund, that donation *does* take some cash. Half that cash may well be money that would have gone to the IRS; but half of it would otherwise have been available to finance growth in the business! When money is put into the pension and profit-sharing trust fund, or is given as bonuses to employees, it's *gone*—and it's *not* available to finance growth.

Say the sum of money that is likely to be left in the business from operations for the coming year is expected to be 2 percent (after taxes, *after adjustments)* on sales volume. This is a very realistic (actually on the high side) profit percentage according to the average profitability of companies reported in the Robert Morris Associates Annual Statement Studies. While some may say that 2 percent on net sales is low, remember that this is the after-tax, after-adjustments return on sales. In fact, the 2-percent figure is actually high for the average business (albeit low for many truly high-profitability firms).

Two percent of $12,500,000 (next year's expected annual sales volume) is $250,000. So we have $250,000 from anticipated retained earnings to use toward the required $1,250,000 needed to finance our expected sales volume increase.

We Now Subtract Our Depreciation Schedule

The next source of cash to finance growth is the depreciation schedule expected for the coming year. Use caution when looking at the depreciation schedule. Many corporate planners automatically assume that depreciation provides cash for cash flow and growth operations in a firm, but this is not necessarily true. Depreciation provides cash *if* the company is profitable. If the company is not profitable, the depreciation does not provide cash, because depreciation gives the company an opportunity to make a bookkeeping expense entry on the profit-and-loss statement for which a check does not have to be issued. This is why depreciation must also be net of loan principle repayments. Checks *are* issued for loan principle repayments, but no bookkeeping entry on the profit-and-loss statement is made for such payments, causing the reverse effect of depreciation. Therefore, depreciation net of loan principle repayments provides money to the operational revenues of the firm—but this *only* occurs if the company is profitable. If depreciation charges for a business are $400,000 for a year, and the business loses $600,000, it means that the business only has an actual cash shortfall of $200,000. The additional bookkeeping entry of "Depreciation Expense" of $400,000 simply runs up the loss, but does *not* provide cash.

Suppose, however, that the company is profitable. After making year-end adjustments and paying taxes, you still report an income of $250,000. Therefore, the depreciation schedule will also provide cash because you were profitable.

If a firm has approximately $6,250,000 in assets (which is where we'll be at the close of the forthcoming year), they will probably have a depreciation schedule somewhere in the neighborhood of $250,000. Only approximately $2–$2.5 million in a total asset base of $6,250,000 is apt to be in depreciable assets. And a 10-percent total depreciable asset figure is fairly realistic and normal.

So now we've provided another $250,000 of cash with which to finance growth. To recap the score: The required financing for growth is $1,250,000. Earnings provide $250,000. The depreciation schedule provides $250,000. We're only three quarters of a million dollars short.

Investment Tax Credits Also Provide Cash

One other source of cash used to finance growth is any investment tax credits available to the firm for the anticipated year. The investment tax credit provides us with cash because, like depreciation, it permits us to avoid sending a check to the IRS.

A business that is going to accumulate another $1,250,000 in assets will probably accumulate something on the order of $300,000–$400,000 in fixed assets that are depreciable and that may come under the investment tax credit. This means that there is somewhere in the neighborhood of $25,000 made available to finance the growth of the firm in the form of investment tax credits.

So now we can deduct another $25,000 from the remaining $750,000 needed to finance our growth. That leaves us now with a $725,000 shortfall. And it also comes to the end of our formula, because there isn't any other source of cash generated by the business. So we're left with a $725,000 shortfall in cash required to finance growth if everything comes through as anticipated (and as is normal for the typical manufacturing firm).

But We Can Borrow Money

The only other alternative is to borrow money. We can just borrow $725,000 from the bank, trade creditors, suppliers, or vendors.

Financing growth is either going to come from additional debt to whatever source (bank, suppliers, vendors, etc.) or from equity money that must be put into the business. There's one way to determine whether or not there is sufficient borrowing capability for the firm to borrow the money needed. Take the formula:

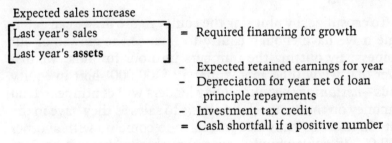

Expected sales increase

$$\left[\frac{\text{Last year's sales}}{\text{Last year's \textbf{assets}}} \right] = \text{Required financing for growth}$$

- Expected retained earnings for year
- Depreciation for year net of loan principle repayments
- Investment tax credit
- = Cash shortfall if a positive number

Now change the asset figure to the equity figure in the business. If we do that the formula looks as follows:

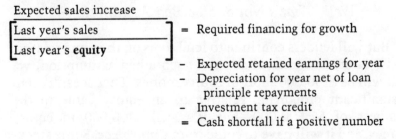

Expected sales increase

$$\left[\frac{\text{Last year's sales}}{\text{Last year's \textbf{equity}}} \right] = \text{Required financing for growth}$$

- Expected retained earnings for year
- Depreciation for year net of loan principle repayments
- Investment tax credit
- = Cash shortfall if a positive number

By changing the asset portion of the formula to read "equity," the amount of equity required to finance the growth of the business can be determined—assuming, of course, that our money lenders (bankers, suppliers, vendors, etc.) will *continue* to lend to us on the same relative rate they have in the past. They may—but then, they may not, too.

Substituting into our formula, we can figure out if our borrowing capacity is indeed sufficient to fund our growth without putting in additional equity. An equity figure of approximately half our asset base is reasonable, using a rough average from the Robert Morris Associates Annual Statement Studies figures, which show that the typical manufacturer usually has about $1 debt for every dollar of net worth or equity found in the business. In other words, they usually have a debt-to-worth ratio of 1:1. Therefore, if we plug in the appropriate numbers to include an equity figure of $2,500,000, we find the following formulation:

$$\frac{\$\ 2,500,000}{\begin{bmatrix} \$10,000,000 \\ \$\ 2,500,000 \end{bmatrix}} = \$625,000 - \$250,000 - \$250,000 - \$25,000 = \$100,000$$

To capsulize, by plugging the equity figure in, we can determine if we have enough equity to finance the growth of our business. By putting the numbers into our formula, we discover that we will be approximately $100,000 short in equity funds—*assuming* that our money lenders will continue to lend us money on the same relative basis to sales as they have in the past. So now we know we will have to come up with another $100,000 in equity funds—even though our business has had fairly high profitability.

Well, That's Not Such a Bad Assumption

But will lenders continue to lend to us on the same relative basis? First, assuming that's not such a bad assumption, we still will be $100,000 short in equity money. That doesn't seem a significant proportion relative to an equity value in the business of $2,500,000—but it's still $100,000 in equity money, and it will have to come from *some place*. Some stockholder will have to be assessed, or some stock will have to be sold off; something will have to be done to raise it. But we can probably come up with it somewhere.

The second problem is whether our money lenders *will* continue to lend to us on the same relative rate they have in the past. But this is *not* a valid assumption if we look at past history.

An analysis of the Robert Morris Associates 1980 Annual Statement Studies show the following probabilities, by class of industry, of whether or not money lenders might be willing to continue to lend money on the same relative basis as the business grows. It is, in fact, *not* a likely probability for manufacturers, wholesalers, or retailers. Only the service and construction industry classifications have that likelihood available to them. And they, quantity-wise, represent a very insignificant percentage of businesses when one considers all the classifications represented in the studies.

This break-out, which I will call debt-to-worth ratio for the businesses, can be classified as follows:

Manufacturing Industry

In 79 out of 131 cases, the debt-to-worth ratio *decreases* as the businesses grow. This means that as businesses get bigger, their ability to sustain their relative rate of borrowing goes down, not up as most people assume.

In only 20 out of 131 cases does the debt-to-worth ratio go up as manufacturing businesses grow. Better not count on being able to borrow at the same relative rate.

Wholesalers

In 22 out of 57 cases, the debt-to-worth ratio *decreases* as the businesses increase in size. In 27 out of 57 cases, the debt-to-worth ratio goes up. Here your chances of borrowing at the same relative rate are a little over 50 percent.

Retailers

In 24 out of 49 cases, the debt-to-worth ratio *decreases* as retailing businesses grow. In 23 out of 49 cases, the debt-to-worth ratio goes up as the retailer grows in sales volume. Again, you are looking at about a 50-percent probability of being able to borrow at the same relative rate.

Service Industries

In 14 out of 48 cases, the debt-to-worth ratio *decreases* as the service industry grows. In 32 out of 48 instances, the debt-to-worth ratio goes up as the service industry grows. Therefore, in the service industry one can probably expect to be able to borrow at the same relative rate as the business gets bigger, or possibly even borrow at a higher rate.

Contracting Industries

In 4 out of 18 cases, the debt-to-worth ratio *decreases* as the contractor grows in sales volume. In 11 out of 18 cases, the debt-to-worth ratio goes up as the contracting business grows. The contractor, too, can expect to borrow amply as the contracting business grows.

So Another Truth Fails Us

Once again we see a myth of management that proves to be not true. Again, relative to sales and to total assets, money lenders *don't* seem to be any more sympathetic to larger businesses than they are to small businesses. This, obviously, is why the larger businesses end up having to go into the money markets to get cash. And the money market that they prefer to go to, in order to finance their growth, often is the source of nonrepayable debt—which is another way of saying selling off stock or equity in the business.

It simply is not true that most businesses can generate enough money to finance their own growth; while it is true that some can, the overwhelming majority cannot. This is why there is such a strong demand for equity funds in American business and industry.

Raising funds is simply one more job of the professional manager of a large corporation. But the owner/manager may look at it differently. Like Henry Ford, many people want to build a business and own it themselves. But the problem is, it becomes progressively difficult as the business increases in size to continue to maintain growth from funds generated from business operations.

27

Summary and Conclusions

This book has dealt with truth in management. We began talking about truth in managing oneself—if you want a job done right, do it yourself; hard work never hurt anyone; idle hands are the workshop of the devil. Then we progressed through truth in leadership and analyzed beliefs such as the open-door policy, nice guys finish last, a good boss is a good human relator. We analyzed truth in managing others, truth in motivation, truth in selling things, and finally truth in production and finance.

Most of the material here suggests that conventional, accepted wisdom or truth is *not* very true, after all, in the real world of business operations.

My intention has not been to ridicule any particular philosophy or ideology. It was simply to point out that some seemingly basic "truths" simply don't hold water in real work situations. What I did intend to do was to get your gray matter thinking about business management, perhaps in some way slightly different from the conventional viewpoint. If I have caused you to rethink some of the "unarguable" truths in management, I have accomplished my purpose.

You are now invited to retake the Managerial Truth Test on page 5 of Chapter 1.

Bibliography

Human Relations: People and Work (New York: Harper & Row, Publishers), 1979.

First Line Management, 3rd Ed. (Dallas, Texas: Business Publications, Inc.), 1983.

Art and Skill of Delegation (Reading, Massachusetts: Addison-Wesley Publishing Co., Inc.), 1976.

Managing the Small Business, 3rd Ed. (Homewood, Illinois: Richard D. Irwin, Inc.), 1982.

Interviewing Skills for Supervisory Personnel (Reading: Massachusetts: Addison-Wesley Publishing Co., Inc.), 1971.

Managing the Marginal and Unsatisfactory Performer (Reading, Massachusetts: Addison-Wesley Publishing Co., Inc.), 1969. Revised Ed. in press.

Labor Law (Tustin, California: Media Masters, Inc.), 1967.

Grass Roots Approach to Industrial Peace (Ann Arbor, Michigan: Bureau of Industrial Relations), 1966.

Index